LATERAL THINKING

W9-AWG-881

LATERAL THINKING

ARCTURUS

INTRODUCTION

Our brain is undoubtedly our greatest asset, yet for many of us it is the part of the body we tend to take most for granted. We might eat the right foods and take regular exercise to keep us in shape physically, but we do little to maintain or indeed improve our brainpower.

Now's your chance to change this and develop a capacity for thinking that will greatly increase your ability to solve seemingly intractable problems.

Whether you are more creative than logical or vice versa, the enjoyable challenges presented in this superlative compendium will have you thinking outside the box.

WHAT'S IN THIS BOOK

Lateral Thinking includes a mixture of three categories of puzzles and challenges, indicated by symbols. The puzzles enable various types of mental activity to be developed and in the process smooth out left- or right-sided brain bias.

The three categories are:

PUZZLES TO INCREASE LEFT-SIDE BRAIN FUNCTION

Designed to develop our powers of concentration but requiring no specialized knowledge beyond the ability to think clearly and analytically, as well as to test and strengthen our numerical and/or arithmetic skills.

PUZZLES TO INCREASE RIGHT-SIDE BRAIN FUNCTION

Designed to develop our creative potential, these puzzles have the capacity to change our natural or traditional perceptions and help us to find solutions to unusual or especially challenging problems.

PUZZLES TO INCREASE WHOLE-BRAIN FUNCTION

Memory is an essential brain function, and one these puzzles are designed to strengthen. Puzzles involving a high degree of tactical reasoning enhance whole-brain function, and so many of this type are included, too.

TAKE YOUR TIME!

Alongside the puzzles and activities we have provided a timer to prompt you to keep track of how long it takes you to complete each task. Record your start and finish times on the clock faces. Once you understand the solving process you should notice that it takes you less time to complete a particular type of puzzle.

SOLVING THE PUZZLES

Not all of the puzzles will be familiar to you, so on the following pages we have provided an explanation of what is required to complete each puzzle, together with an example of a solved puzzle, where appropriate. But don't worry if you come across puzzles you can't complete – there is a Solutions section at the back of the book.

Progressive Matrix

In each puzzle, draw the contents of the missing tile in accordance with the rules of logic already established.

Here is an example:

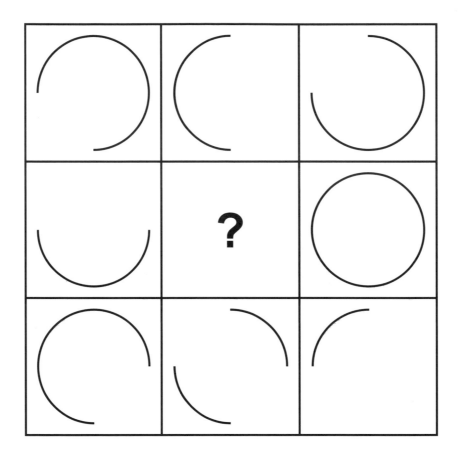

Solution

Looking at lines across and down, the third tile is produced by combining the contents of the first two tiles, except where two lines or symbols appear in the same position in the first two tiles, in which case they are cancelled out.

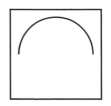

Odd One Out

Study the shapes carefully. Which is the odd one out?

Here is an example:

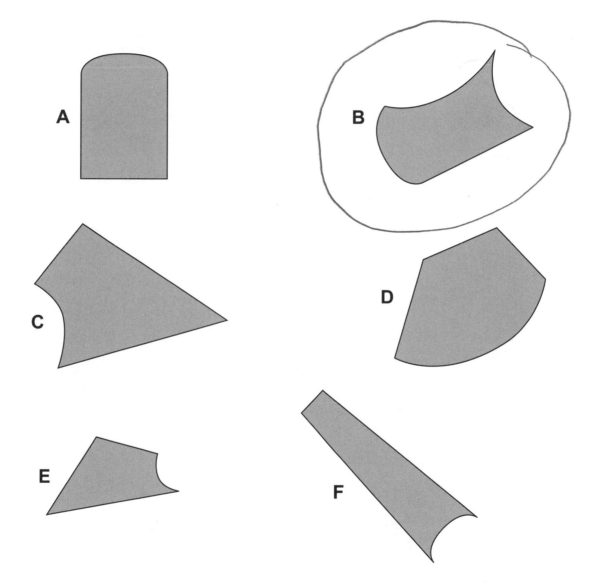

Solution

B – It has three curved sides, the others have only one.

In Sequence

Study the sequence carefully. Which of the alternatives should take the place of the question mark?

Here is an example:

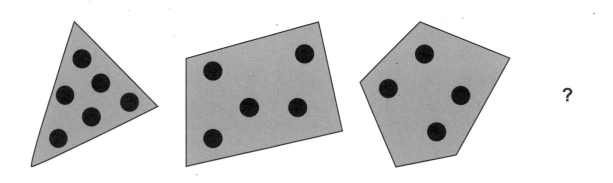

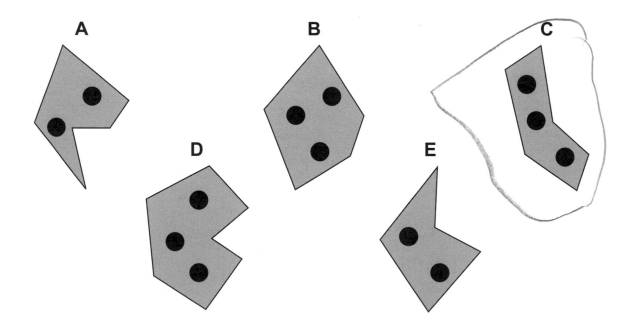

Solution

C – The number of sides in each figure increases by one each time and the number of circles reduces by one each time.

Creative Thinking and Co-ordination

Drawing a copy of a picture is a creative thinking right-brain exercise and involves a great deal of eye and hand co-ordination, especially when drawing in mirror-image.

No solution is given to this task, as it is up to you to decide whether the picture you draw looks accurate. The object of the exercise is to co-ordinate your hand to produce what your eyes see.

Here is an example:

Folding Cubes

Being able to envisage how a flat shape might look when folded is another form of creative thinking right-brain exercise as it involves being able to visualise a three-dimensional shape, from an image that is present only in two-dimensional format.

Here is an example:

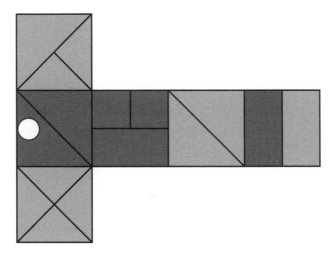

When the above is folded to form a cube, which is the only one of the following that can be produced?

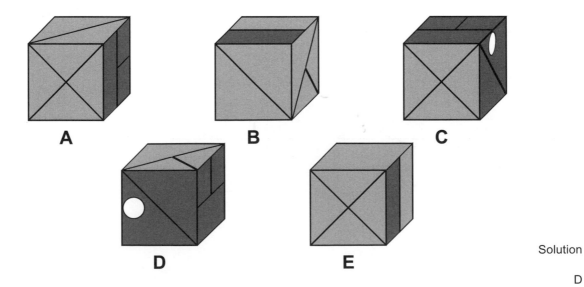

A   **B**   **C**

D   **E**

Solution

D

Memory

Study each puzzle for the number of minutes shown, then turn to the page number shown next to the timer, answering the question(s) that you find there. For the solution, turn back to the original page and check your answer.

Here is an example, indicating that you would need to study the puzzle for two minutes:

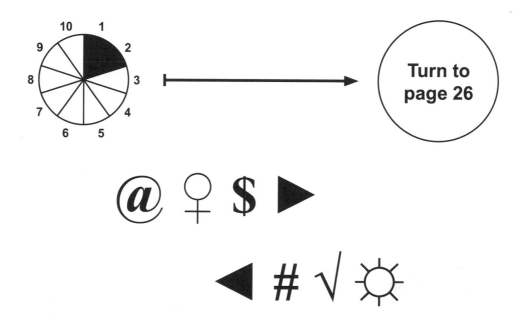

and on page 26:

Which two symbols have changed places?

Tile Twister

Place the eight tiles into the grid so that all adjacent numbers on each tile match up. Any tile may be rotated, but no tile may be flipped over.

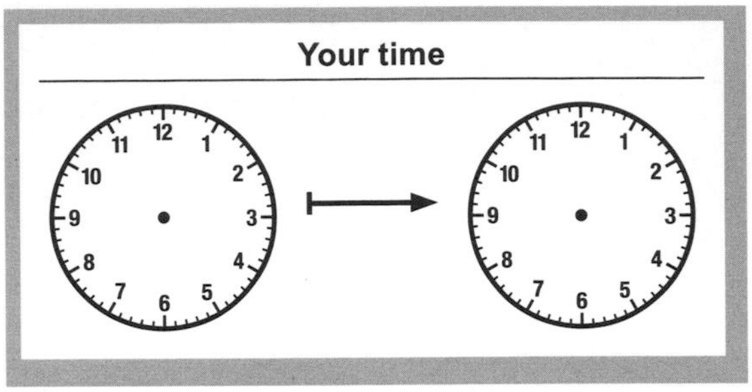

3	3
4	2

2	1
2	4

2	3
2	1

4	1
4	3

2	4
4	1

2	1
4	2

3	4
2	3

4	2
4	1

		2	1		
		1	3		

L-Shaped

Three pieces of each of the four kinds of shape shown below need to be inserted into the grid. Any piece may be turned or flipped over before being put in the grid. No pieces of the same kind can touch, even at a corner. Can you mark in where the Ls are?

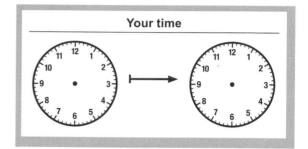

Your time

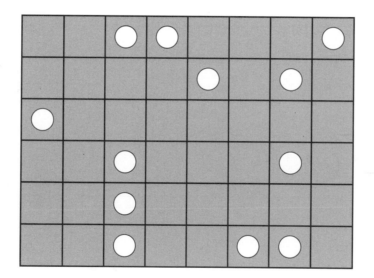

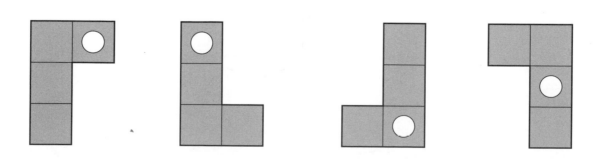

Progressive Matrix

Draw the contents of the missing tile in accordance with the rules of logic already established.

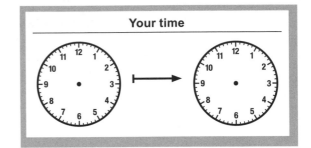

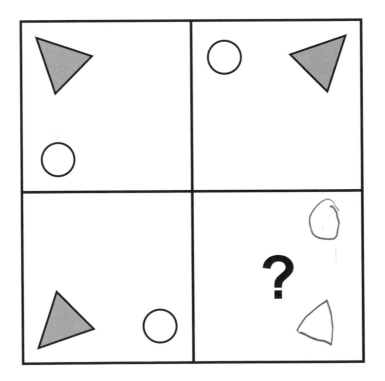

Odd One Out

Study the shapes carefully. Which is the odd one out?

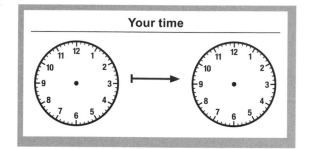

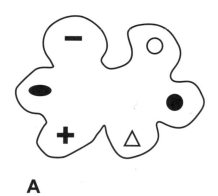

A

B

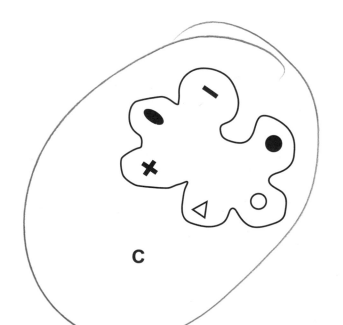

C

D

In Sequence

Study the sequence carefully. Which of the alternatives should take the place of the question mark?

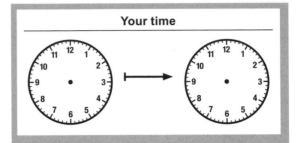

Your time

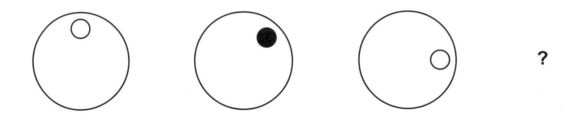

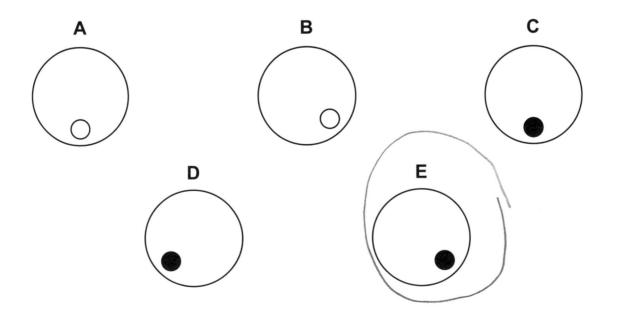

A

B

C

D

E

Folding Cubes

When the shape below is folded to form a cube, which is the only one of the following that can be produced?

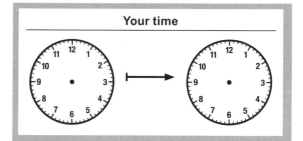

Your time

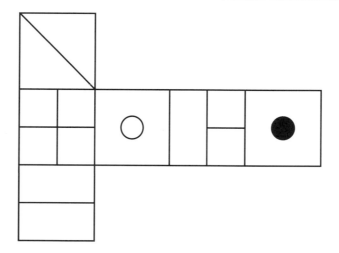

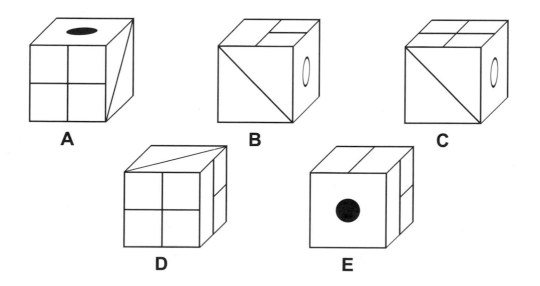

A   B   C

D   E

Memory

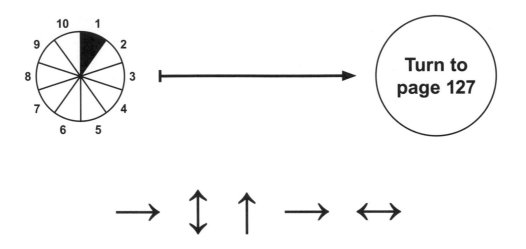

Turn to page 127

Memory

Puzzle 91

Which of the following four numbers appear next to each other in the same order in the sequence?

1 0 8 7	2 4 6 4
9 8 9 2	2 5 6 4

Tile Twister

Place the eight tiles into the grid so that all adjacent numbers on each tile match up. Any tile may be rotated, but no tile may be flipped over.

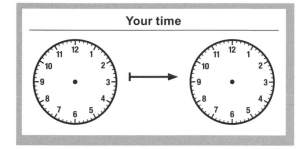

1	1
3	1

3	2
4	1

1	3
3	4

3	4
3	1

2	3
1	1

3	3
1	3

4	2
2	1

1	3
1	4

		2	1		
		4	3		

L-Shaped

Three pieces of each of the four kinds of shape shown below need to be inserted into the grid. Any piece may be turned or flipped over before being put in the grid. No pieces of the same kind can touch, even at a corner. Can you mark in where the Ls are?

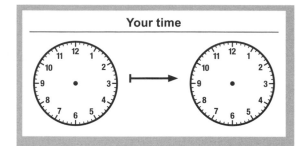

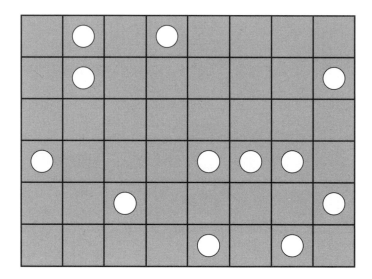

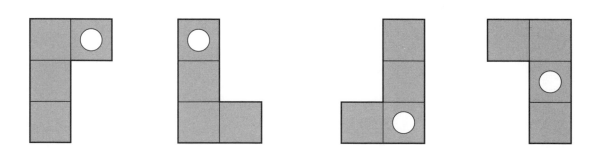

Progressive Matrix

Draw the contents of the missing tile in accordance with the rules of logic already established.

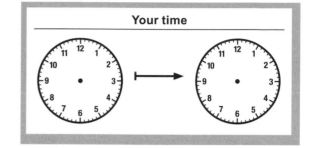

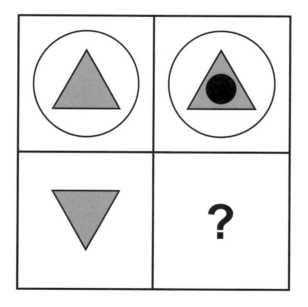

Odd One Out

Study the shapes carefully. Which is the odd one out?

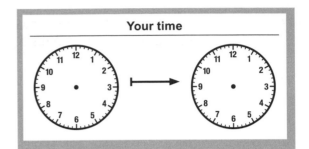

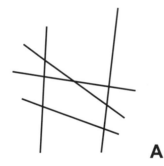

A

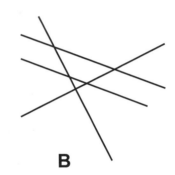

B

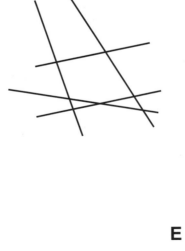

C

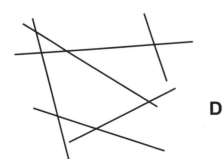

D

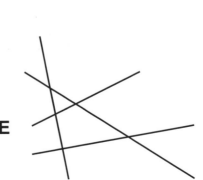

E

In Sequence

Study the sequence carefully. Which of the alternatives should take the place of the question mark?

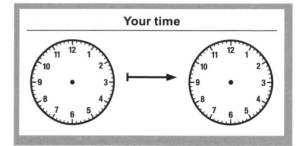

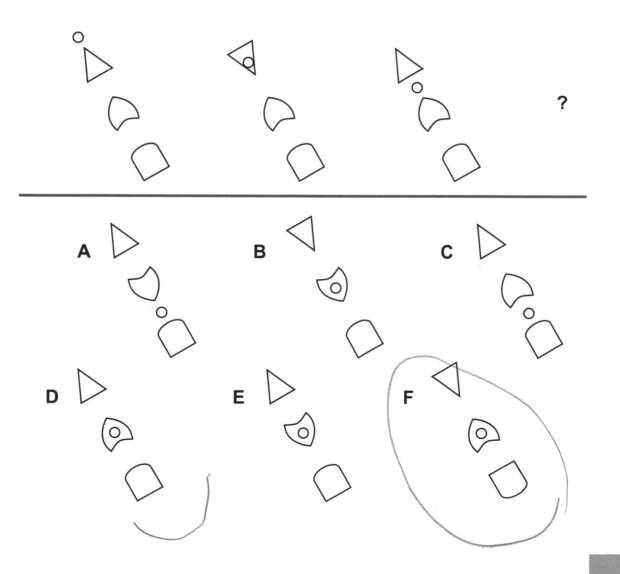

?

A

B

C

D

E

F

Folding Cubes

When the shape below is folded to form a cube, which is the only one of the following that can be produced?

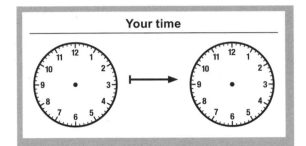

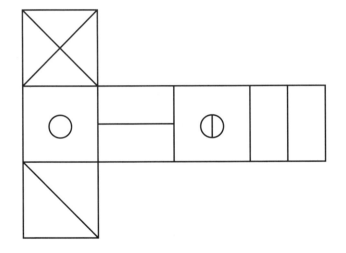

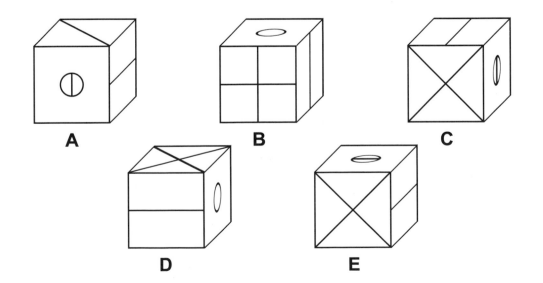

Memory

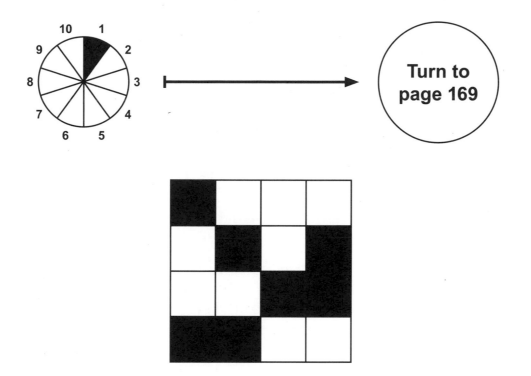

Turn to page 169

Memory

Puzzle 126

Answer the questions below.

Which letter begins and ends the second row?

Which letter appears twice in the third row?

Which letter appears in the middle of the top row?

Tile Twister

Place the eight tiles into the grid so that all adjacent numbers on each tile match up. Any tile may be rotated, but no tile may be flipped over.

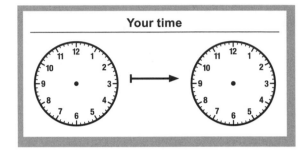

Your time

2	3
3	1

3	2
2	1

4	1
1	3

2	1
3	3

2	2
4	3

1	2
3	2

4	1
4	2

4	4
4	1

		4	3		
		1	3		

L-Shaped

Three pieces of each of the four kinds of shape shown below need to be inserted into the grid. Any piece may be turned or flipped over before being put in the grid. No pieces of the same kind can touch, even at a corner. Can you mark in where the Ls are?

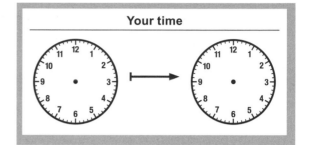

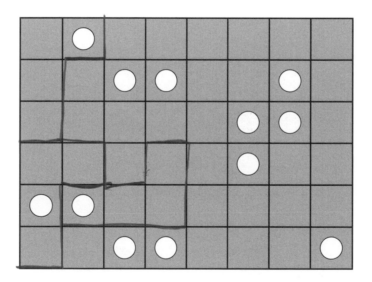

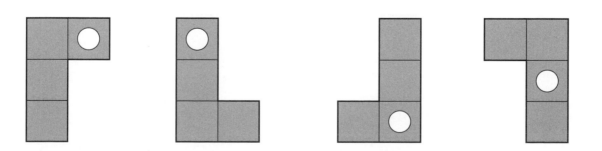

Progressive Matrix

Draw the contents of the missing tile in accordance with the rules of logic already established.

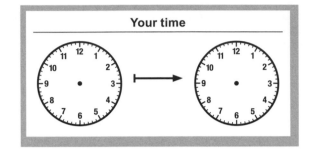

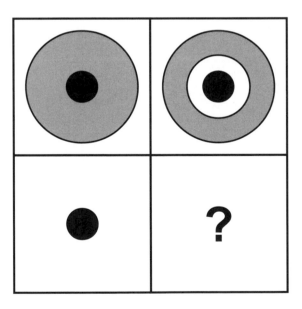

Odd One Out

Study the shapes carefully. Which is the odd one out?

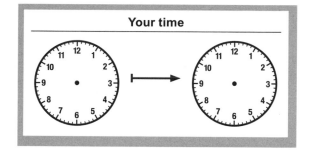

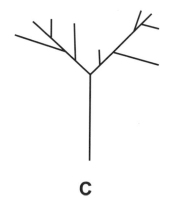

A

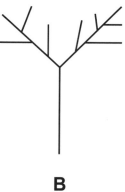

B

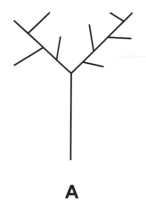

C

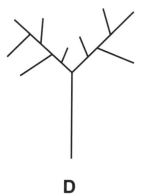

D

In Sequence

Study the sequence carefully. Which of the alternatives should take the place of the question mark?

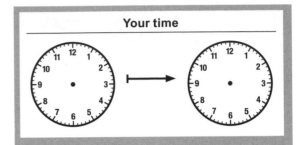

Your time

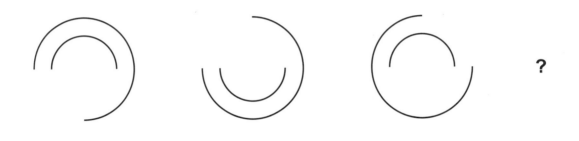

?

A

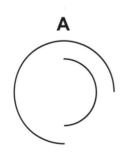

B

C

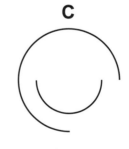

D

E

F

Creative Thinking and Co-ordination

Co-ordinate your hand to produce a mirror image of what your eyes see.

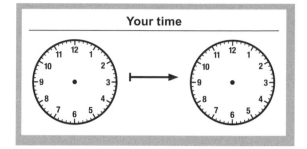

Memory

Turn to page 190

♦ ♫ ☺ ♣ @ #

☼ & ⊥ ∏ ↕ Ω

Memory

Puzzle 77

Answer the questions below.

Which letter was originally in the bottom right corner?

Which symbol has been removed?

Which symbol has changed from black to white?

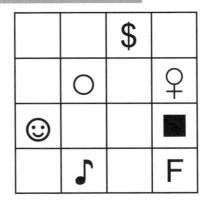

Tile Twister

Place the eight tiles into the grid so that all adjacent numbers on each tile match up. Any tile may be rotated, but no tile may be flipped over.

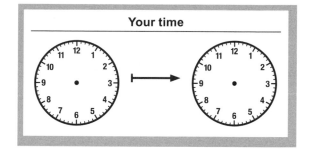

Your time

1	2
3	1

4	1
3	4

3	2
4	2

2	3
4	4

3	4
2	3

2	4
1	3

3	3
1	4

4	2
4	1

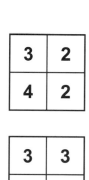

4	1				
2	2				

L-Shaped

Three pieces of each of the four kinds of shape shown below need to be inserted into the grid. Any piece may be turned or flipped over before being put in the grid. No pieces of the same kind can touch, even at a corner. Can you mark in where the Ls are?

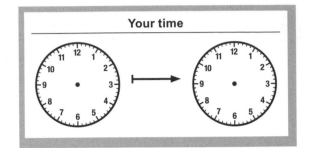

Your time

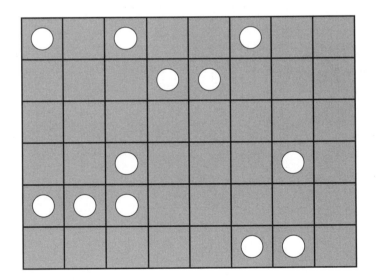

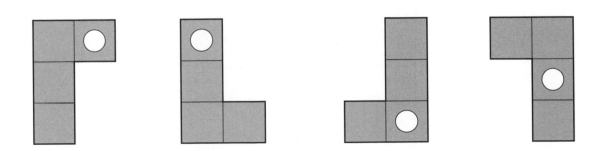

Progressive Matrix

Draw the contents of the missing tile in accordance with the rules of logic already established.

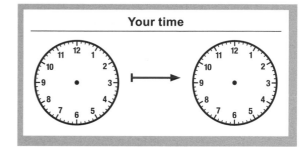

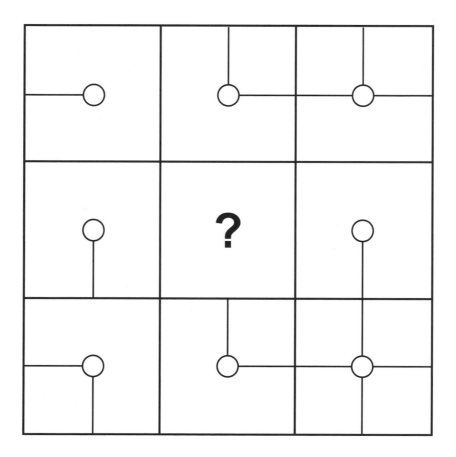

Odd One Out

Study the shapes carefully. Which is the odd one out?

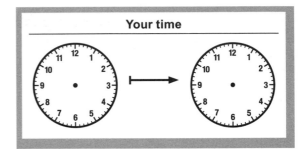

Your time

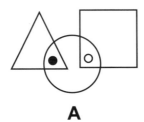

A

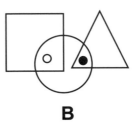

B

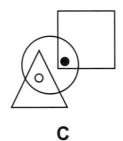

C

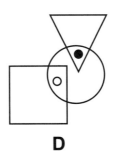

D

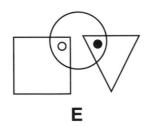

E

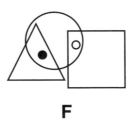

F

In Sequence

Study the sequence carefully. Which of the alternatives should take the place of the question mark?

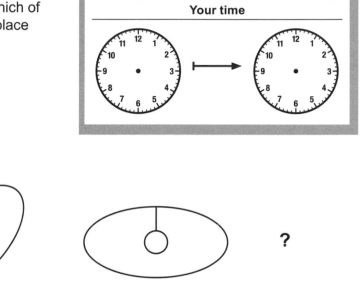

Your time

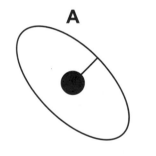 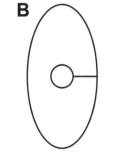 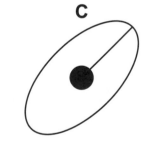 ?

A **B** **C**

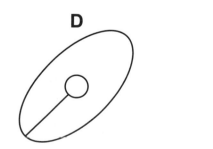

D **E**

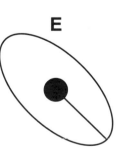

Folding Cubes

When the shape below is folded to form a cube, which is the only one of the following that can be produced?

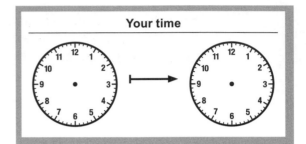

Your time

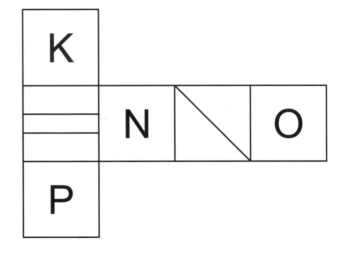

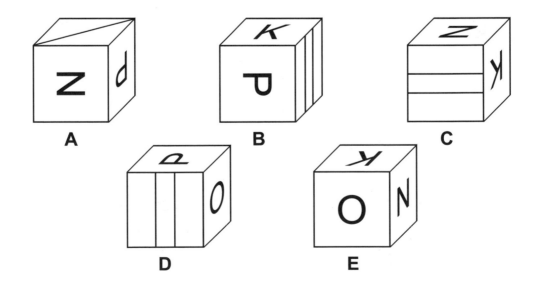

A   B   C

D   E

Memory

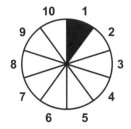

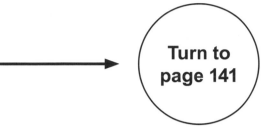

Turn to page 141

Memory

Puzzle 154

Put these into their correct positions:

♣ 7 ♪ ☺ D £ E #

Tile Twister

Place the eight tiles into the grid so that all adjacent numbers on each tile match up. Any tile may be rotated, but no tile may be flipped over.

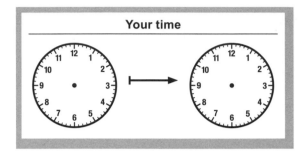

Your time

1	3
2	1

4	1
4	1

2	3
2	1

4	1
2	2

1	3
4	3

1	1
2	4

4	2
3	4

3	3
3	3

Grid:

3	3				
1	2				

L-Shaped

Three pieces of each of the four kinds of shape shown below need to be inserted into the grid. Any piece may be turned or flipped over before being put in the grid. No pieces of the same kind can touch, even at a corner. Can you mark in where the Ls are?

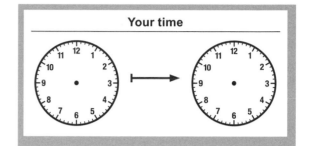

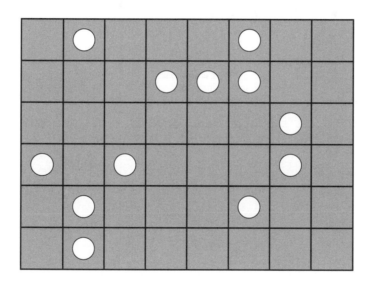

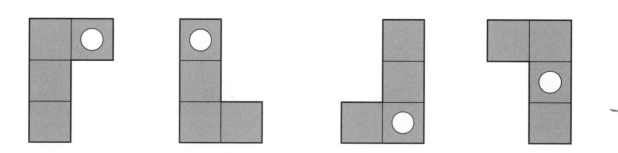

Progressive Matrix

Draw the contents of the missing tile
in accordance with the rules of logic
already established.

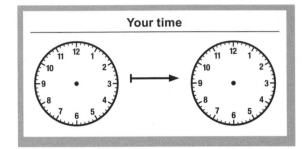

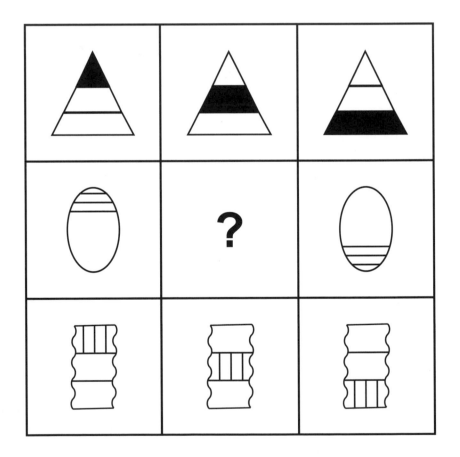

Odd One Out

Study the shapes carefully. Which is the odd one out?

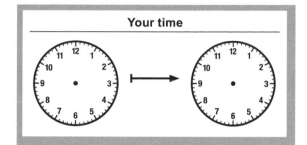

Your time

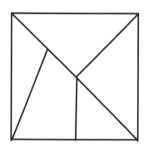

A

B

C

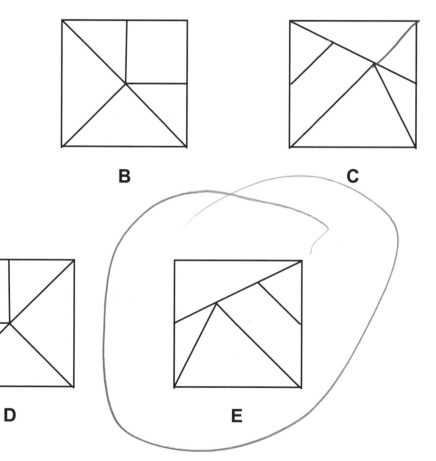

D

E

In Sequence

Study the sequence carefully. Which of the alternatives should take the place of the question mark?

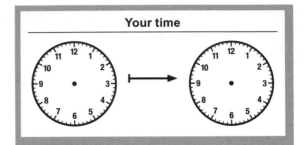
Your time

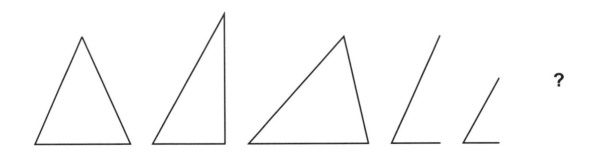

?

A

B

C

D

E

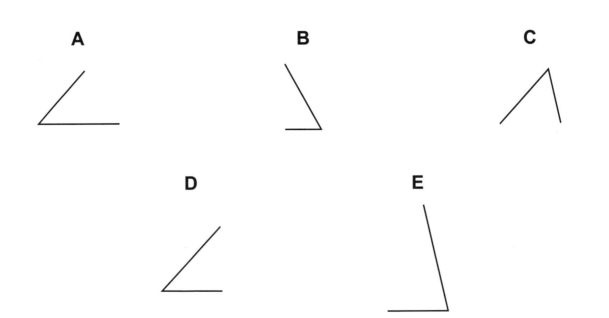

Folding Cubes

When the shape below is folded to form a cube, which is the only one of the following that can be produced?

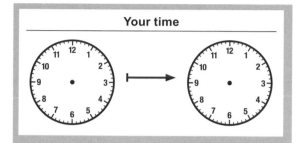

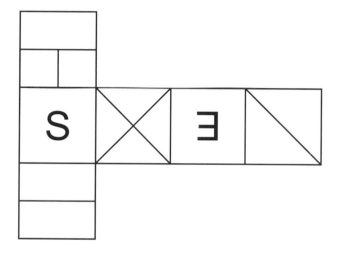

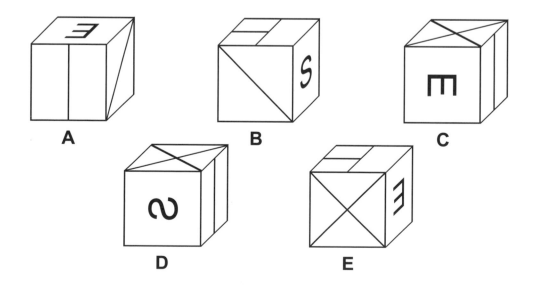

A

B

C

D

E

Memory

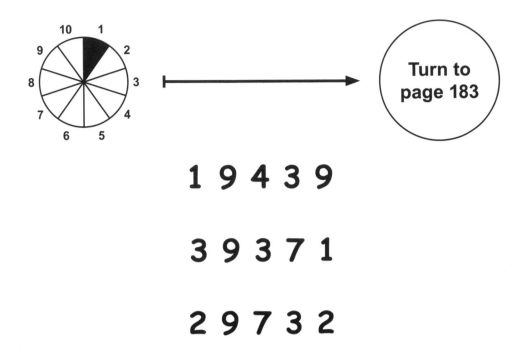

Turn to page 183

1 9 4 3 9

3 9 3 7 1

2 9 7 3 2

Memory

Puzzle 112

Which two symbols have changed places?

Tile Twister

Place the eight tiles into the grid so that all adjacent numbers on each tile match up. Any tile may be rotated, but no tile may be flipped over.

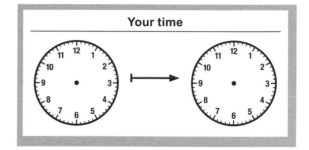

2	4
1	3

3	2
2	4

3	4
1	4

1	2
2	3

4	4
3	2

2	1
3	1

4	2
4	1

4	1
2	4

				3	1
				1	4

L-Shaped

Three pieces of each of the four kinds of shape shown below need to be inserted into the grid. Any piece may be turned or flipped over before being put in the grid. No pieces of the same kind can touch, even at a corner. Can you mark in where the Ls are?

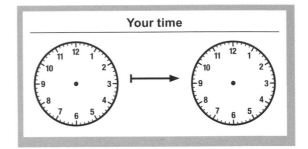

Your time

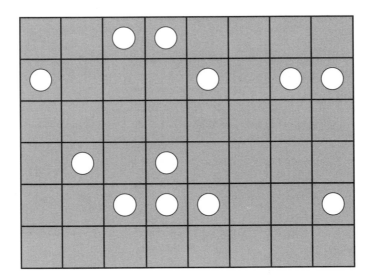

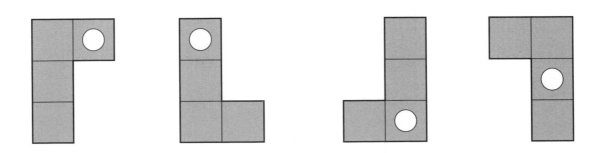

Progressive Matrix

Draw the contents of the missing tile in accordance with the rules of logic already established.

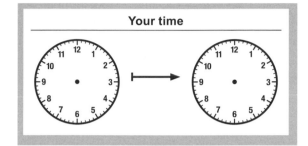

Odd One Out

Study the shapes carefully. Which is the odd one out?

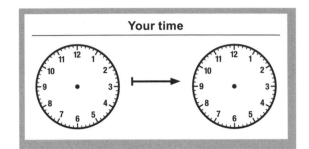

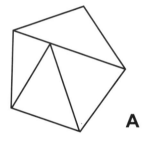

A

B

C

D

E

In Sequence

Study the sequence carefully. Which of the alternatives should take the place of the question mark?

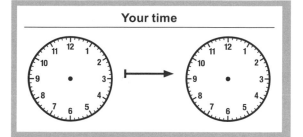

Your time

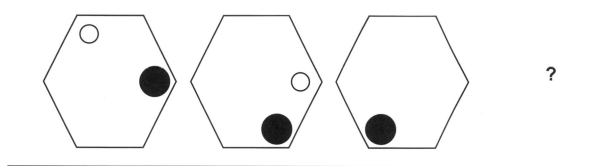

?

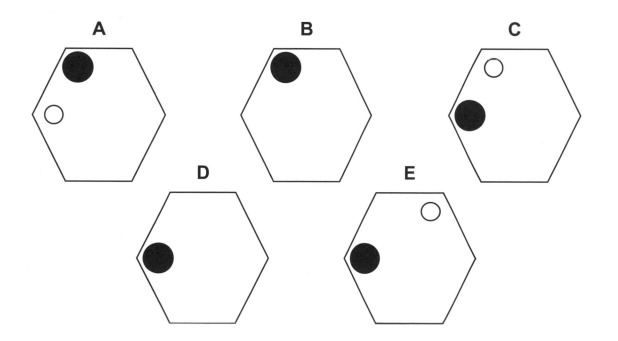

A

B

C

D

E

Creative Thinking and Co-ordination

Co-ordinate your hand to produce a mirror image of what your eyes see.

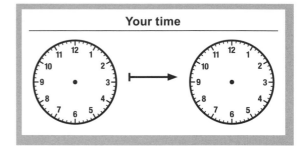

Memory

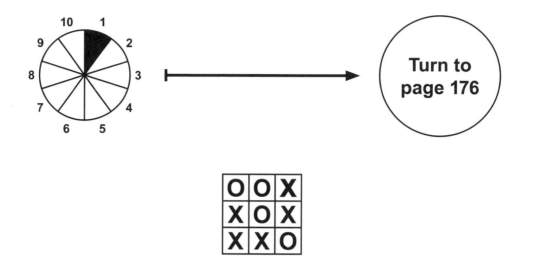

Turn to page 176

O	O	X
X	O	X
X	X	O

Memory

Puzzle 63

Which of these did you see?

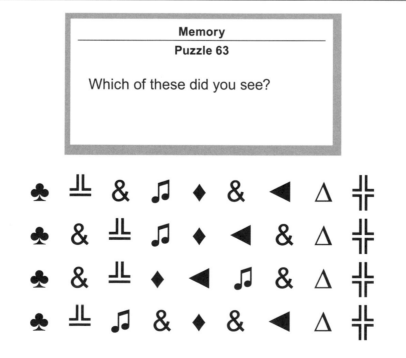

Tile Twister

Place the eight tiles into the grid so that all adjacent numbers on each tile match up. Any tile may be rotated, but no tile may be flipped over.

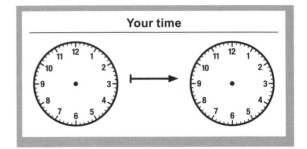

1	2
4	4

4	2
1	2

4	2
2	3

4	1
1	2

1	3
2	2

3	2
4	4

2	3
2	2

3	3
2	1

3	4				
1	2				

L-Shaped

Three pieces of each of the four kinds of shape shown below need to be inserted into the grid. Any piece may be turned or flipped over before being put in the grid. No pieces of the same kind can touch, even at a corner. Can you mark in where the Ls are?

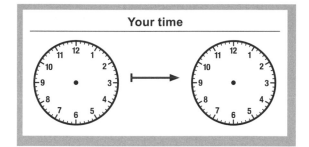

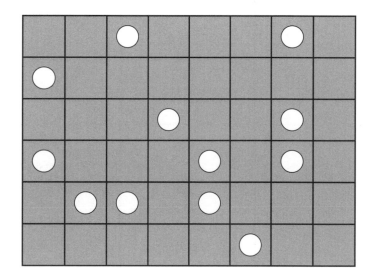

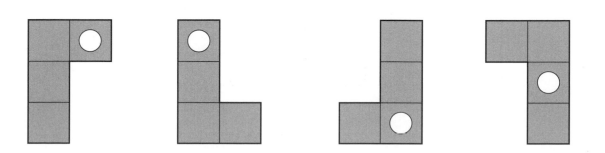

Progressive Matrix

Draw the contents of the missing tile in accordance with the rules of logic already established.

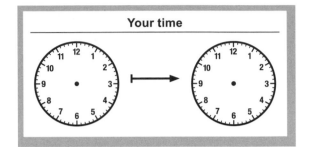

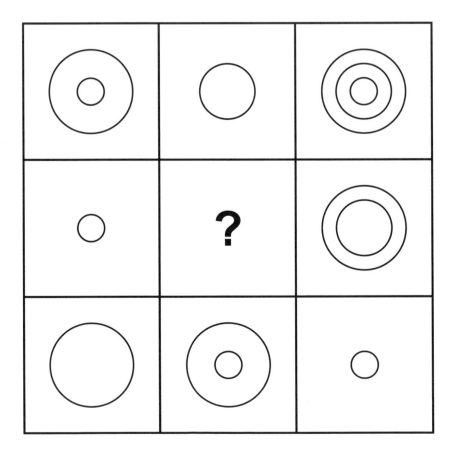

Odd One Out

Study the shapes carefully. Which is the odd one out?

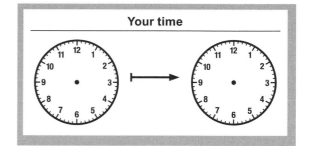

Your time

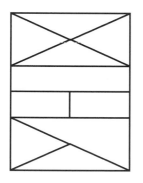

A

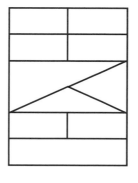

B

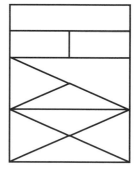

C

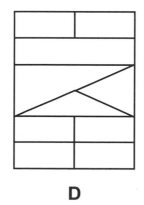

D

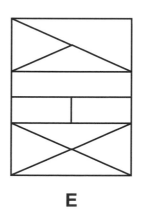

E

In Sequence

Study the sequence carefully. Which of the alternatives should take the place of the question mark?

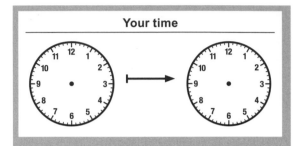

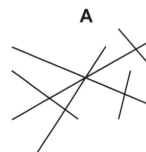

?

A

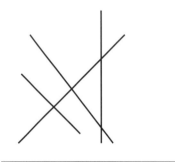

B

C

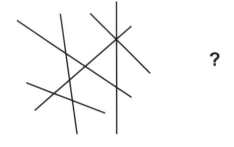

D

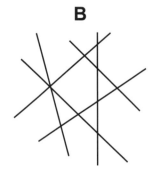

E

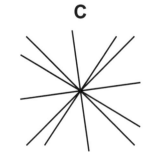

Folding Cubes

When the shape below is folded to form a cube, which is the only one of the following that can be produced?

Your time

A **B** **C**

D **E**

Memory

Turn to
page 148

4 6 3 1 0 1 6 4 9
7 6 2 1 6 4 3 2

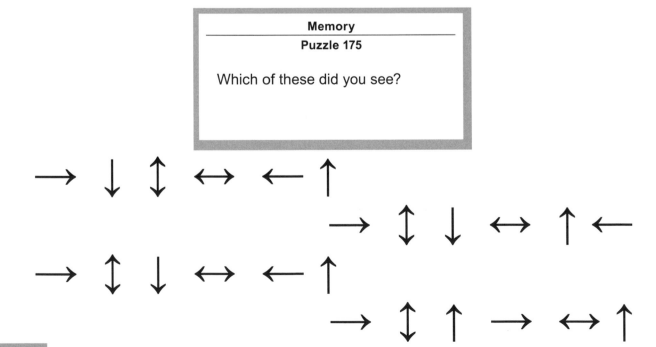

Memory

Puzzle 175

Which of these did you see?

Tile Twister

Place the eight tiles into the grid so that all adjacent numbers on each tile match up. Any tile may be rotated, but no tile may be flipped over.

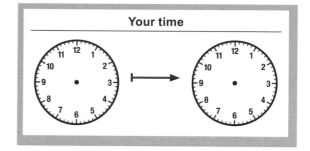

Your time

3	3
4	2

2	2
4	2

1	3
3	1

3	4
2	2

2	2
3	3

3	1
3	2

3	4
3	1

1	3
3	2

1	2		
3	1		

L-Shaped

Three pieces of each of the four kinds of shape shown below need to be inserted into the grid. Any piece may be turned or flipped over before being put in the grid. No pieces of the same kind can touch, even at a corner. Can you mark in where the Ls are?

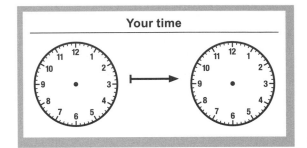

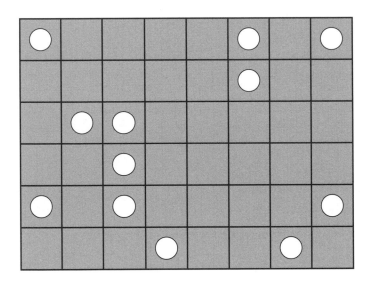

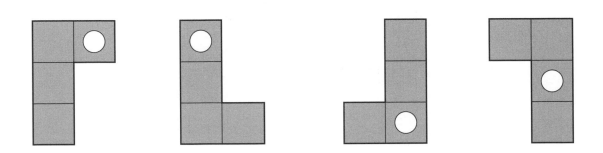

Progressive Matrix

Draw the contents of the missing tile in accordance with the rules of logic already established.

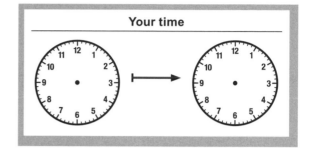

7	9	11
10	13	16
13	17	?

Odd One Out

Study the shapes carefully. Which is the odd one out?

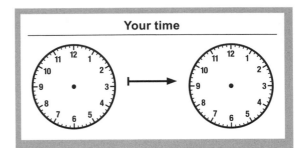

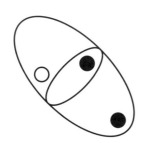

A

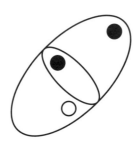

B

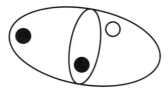

C

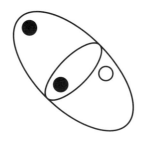

D

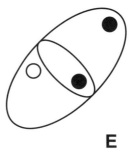

E

In Sequence

Study the sequence carefully. Which of the alternatives should take the place of the question mark?

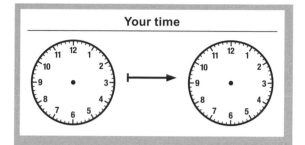

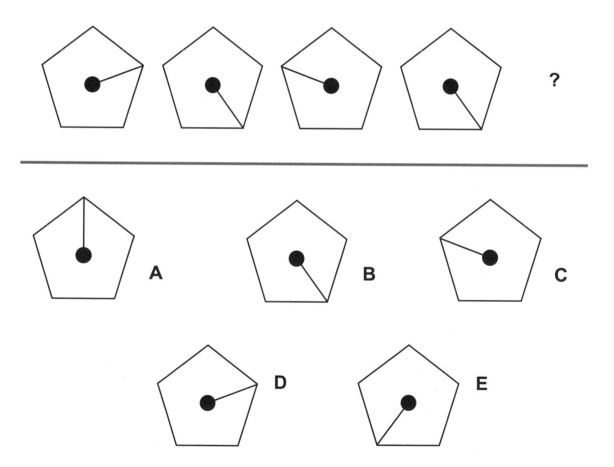

Folding Cubes

When the shape below is folded to form a cube, which is the only one of the following that can be produced?

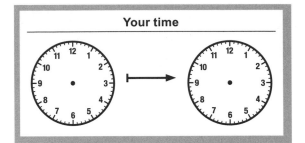

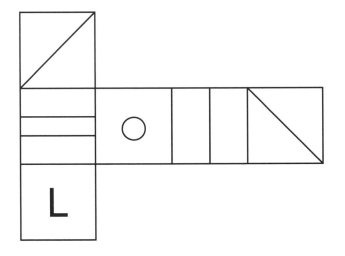

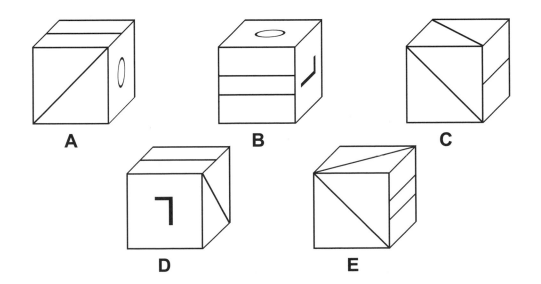

Memory

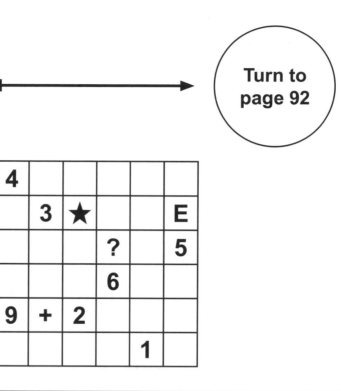

Turn to page 92

Turn to page 92

Memory

Puzzle 140

Which of these did you see?

Tile Twister

Place the eight tiles into the grid so that all adjacent numbers on each tile match up. Any tile may be rotated, but no tile may be flipped over.

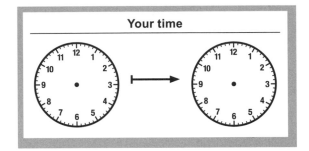

Your time

2	3
1	2

4	4
2	1

3	4
4	3

3	2
1	2

4	4
2	3

4	3
1	1

4	1
3	2

4	2
3	2

				1	1
				4	1

L-Shaped

Three pieces of each of the four kinds of shape shown below need to be inserted into the grid. Any piece may be turned or flipped over before being put in the grid. No pieces of the same kind can touch, even at a corner. Can you mark in where the Ls are?

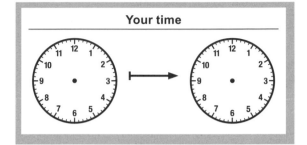

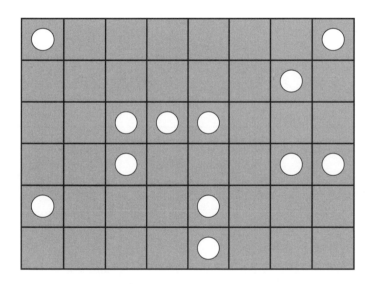

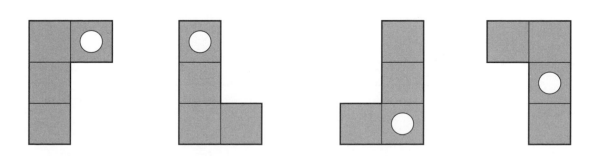

Progressive Matrix

Draw the contents of the missing tile in accordance with the rules of logic already established.

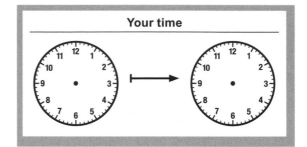

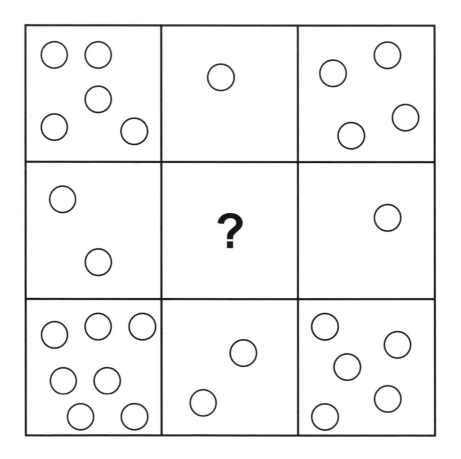

Odd One Out

Study the shapes carefully. Which is the odd one out?

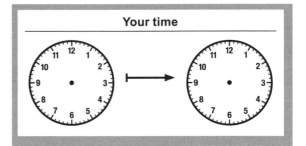

A

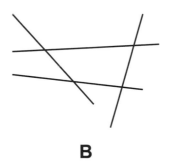

B

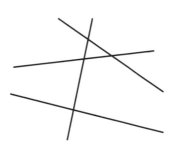

C

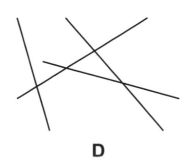

D

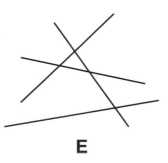

E

In Sequence

Study the sequence carefully. Which of
the alternatives should take the place
of the question mark?

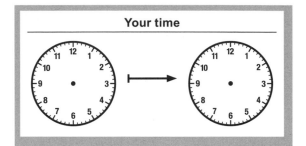

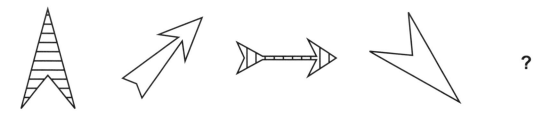

?

A

B

C

D

E

F

G

Creative Thinking and Co-ordination

Co-ordinate your hand to produce a mirror image of what your eyes see.

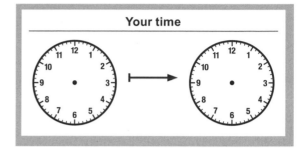

Memory

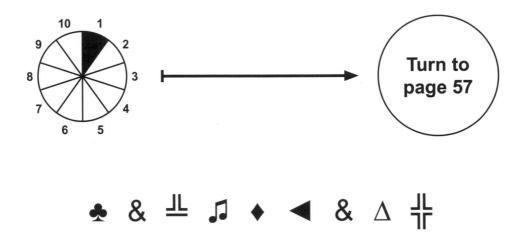

Turn to page 57

♣ & ⊥⊤ ♫ ◆ ◀ & △ ╫

Memory

Puzzle 105

Which of the following are the numbers you have just looked at in reverse?

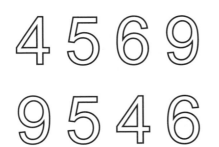

Tile Twister

Place the eight tiles into the grid so that all adjacent numbers on each tile match up. Any tile may be rotated, but no tile may be flipped over.

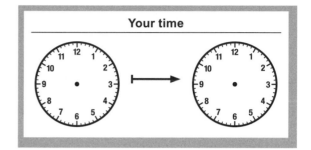

Your time

Tile 1:
4	2
2	1

Tile 2:
4	3
2	3

Tile 3:
2	3
4	1

Tile 4:
1	2
2	3

Tile 5:
3	4
2	2

Tile 6:
4	3
2	4

Tile 7:
1	3
1	3

Tile 8:
2	2
3	1

Grid (with given values):
				1	2
				3	3

L-Shaped

Three pieces of each of the four kinds of shape shown below need to be inserted into the grid. Any piece may be turned or flipped over before being put in the grid. No pieces of the same kind can touch, even at a corner. Can you mark in where the Ls are?

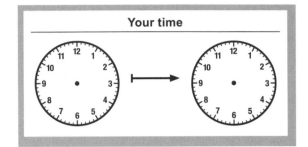

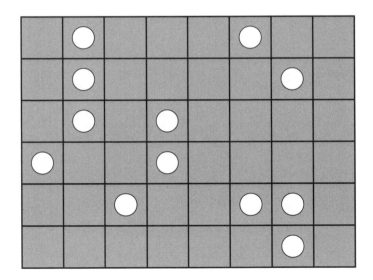

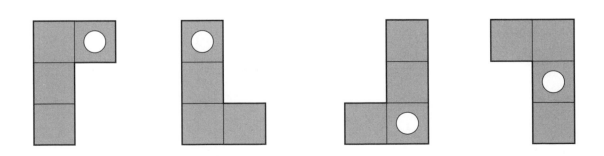

Progressive Matrix

Draw the contents of the missing tile in accordance with the rules of logic already established.

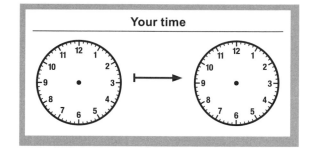

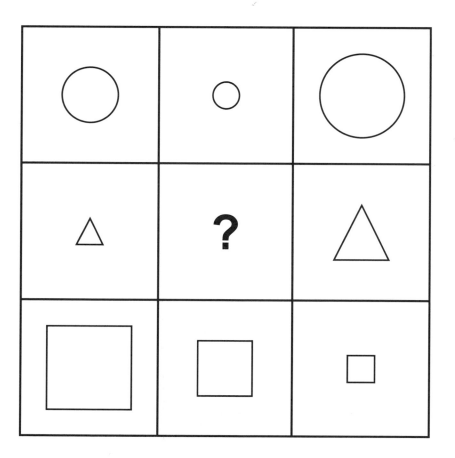

Odd One Out

Study the shapes carefully. Which is the odd one out?

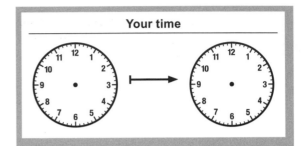

Your time

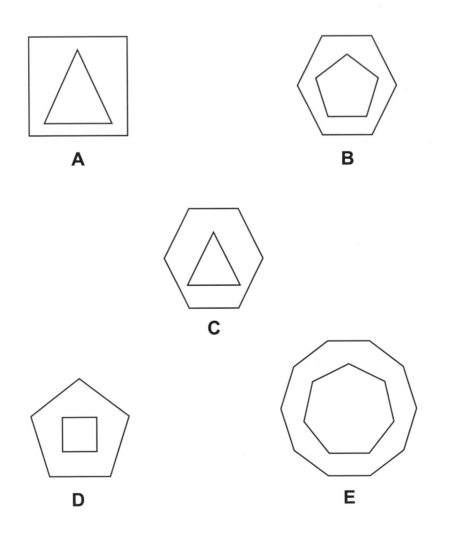

A

B

C

D

E

In Sequence

Study the sequence carefully. Which of the alternatives should take the place of the question mark?

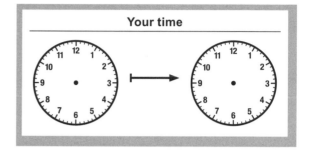

Your time

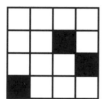   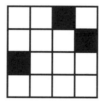   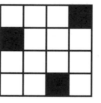

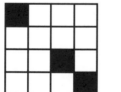   A

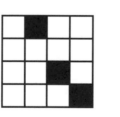   B

C

D

Folding Cubes

When the shape below is folded to form a cube, which is the only one of the following that can be produced?

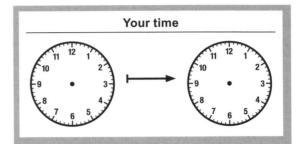

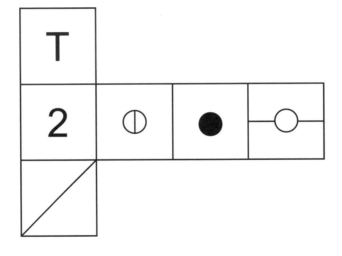

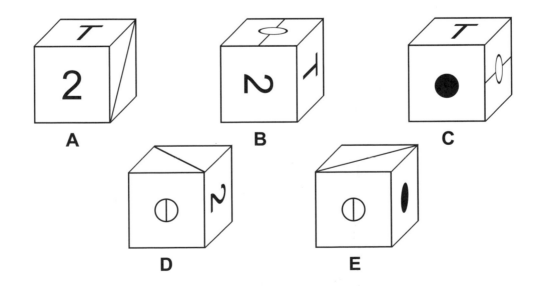

Memory

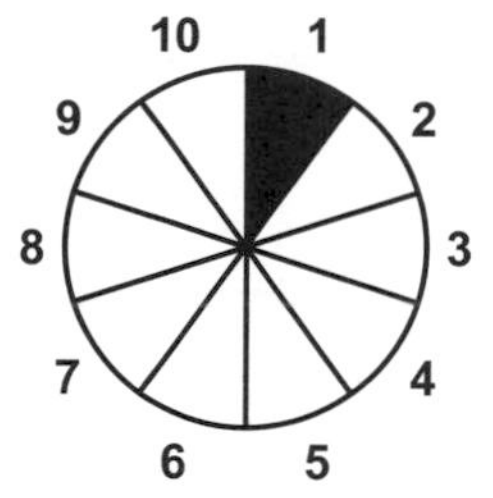

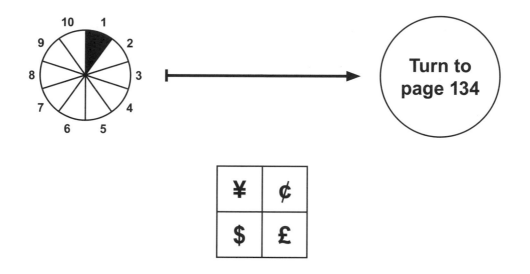

Turn to page 134

¥	¢
$	£

Memory

Puzzle 168

Put these into their correct positions:

Ω £ # 9 M Y D R

Tile Twister

Place the eight tiles into the grid so that all adjacent numbers on each tile match up. Any tile may be rotated, but no tile may be flipped over.

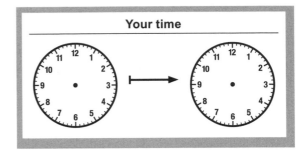

Your time

3	4
4	1

4	2
2	3

3	4
1	1

4	4
3	3

3	2
3	4

4	2
3	4

2	1
4	1

1	4
4	2

1	4				
2	4				

L-Shaped

Three pieces of each of the four kinds of shape shown below need to be inserted into the grid. Any piece may be turned or flipped over before being put in the grid. No pieces of the same kind can touch, even at a corner. Can you mark in where the Ls are?

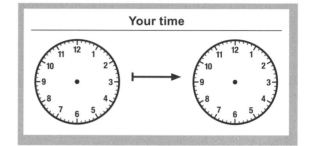

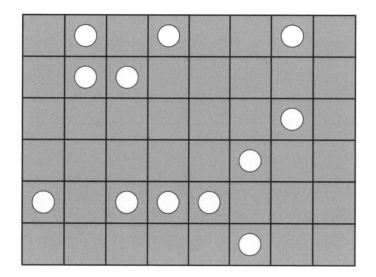

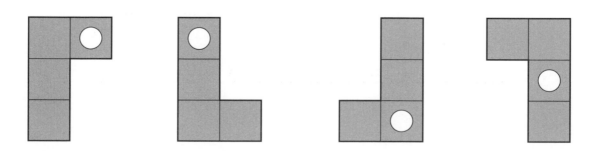

Progressive Matrix

Draw the contents of the missing tile in accordance with the rules of logic already established.

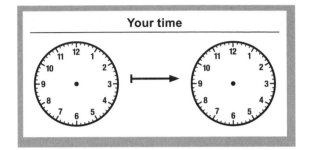

Your time

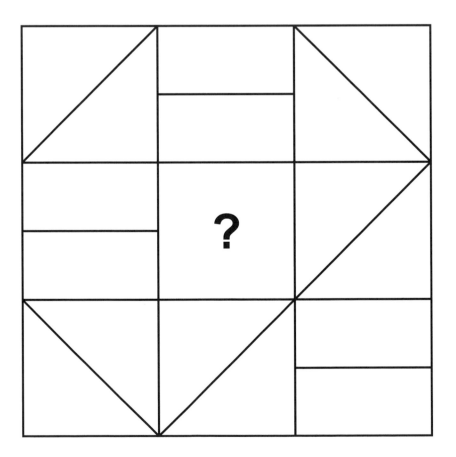

Odd One Out

Study the shapes carefully. Which is the odd one out?

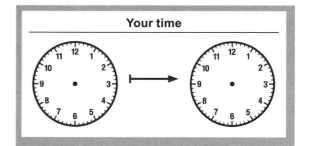

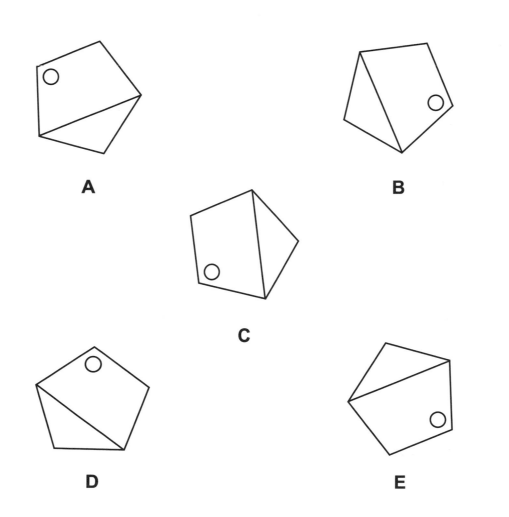

A

B

C

D

E

In Sequence

Study the sequence carefully, then draw the arrow in the circle below, which should take the place of the question mark.

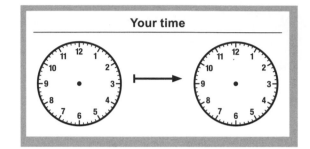

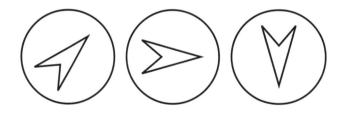 ?

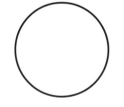

Folding Cubes

When the shape below is folded to form a cube, which is the only one of the following that can be produced?

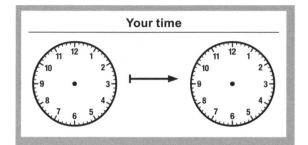

Your time

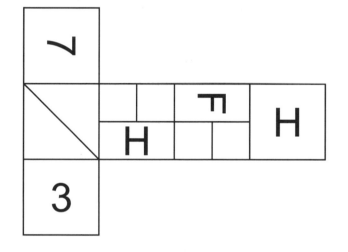

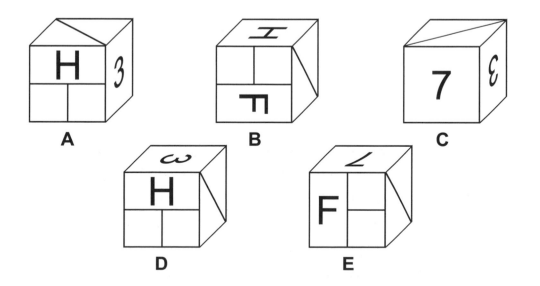

Memory

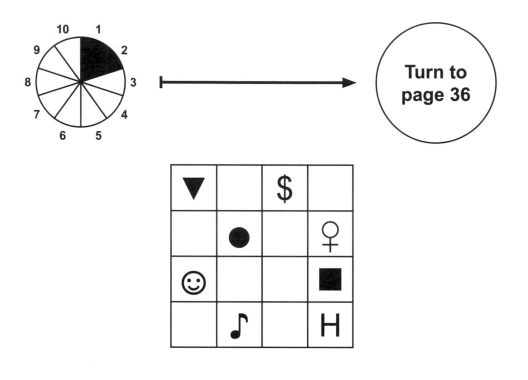

Turn to page 36

Memory

Puzzle 36

Answer the questions below.

What symbol appears immediately to the right of the number 3?

What is the total of the numbers either side of the plus sign?

What number appears in the top left-hand corner?

What number appears immediately below the question mark?

What number appears immediately below the E?

Which is the only number to appear on the bottom line?

Tile Twister

Place the eight tiles into the grid so that all adjacent numbers on each tile match up. Any tile may be rotated, but no tile may be flipped over.

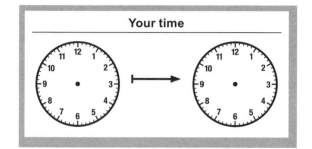

Your time

2	4
3	3

1	2
3	2

3	1
1	4

4	1
3	2

1	2
4	1

3	2
3	1

1	2
2	1

1	3
3	2

				4	3
				1	1

L-Shaped

Three pieces of each of the four kinds of shape shown below need to be inserted into the grid. Any piece may be turned or flipped over before being put in the grid. No pieces of the same kind can touch, even at a corner. Can you mark in where the Ls are?

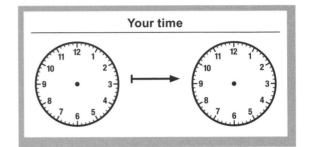

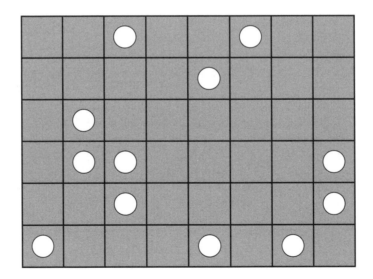

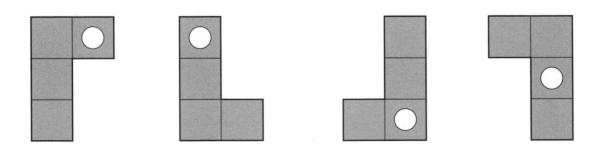

Progressive Matrix

Draw the contents of the missing tile in accordance with the rules of logic already established.

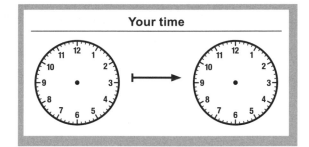

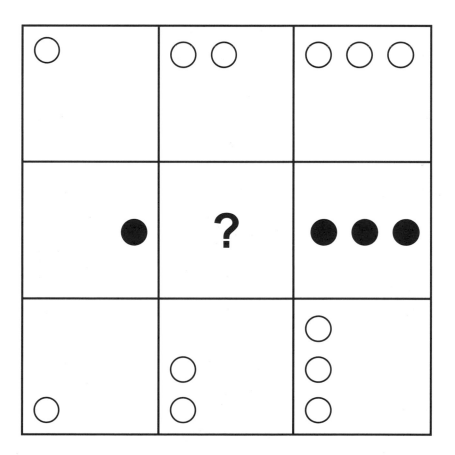

Odd One Out

Study the shapes carefully. Which is the odd one out?

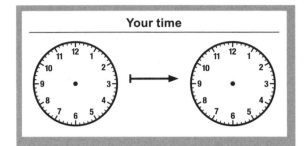

Your time

A

B

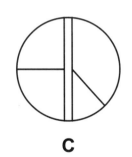

C

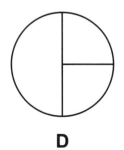

D

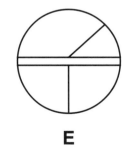

E

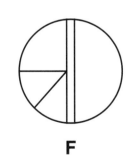

F

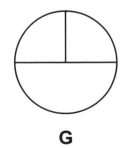

G

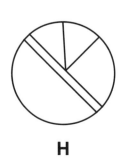

H

I

In Sequence

Study the sequence carefully. Which of the alternatives should take the place of the question mark?

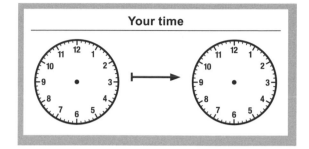

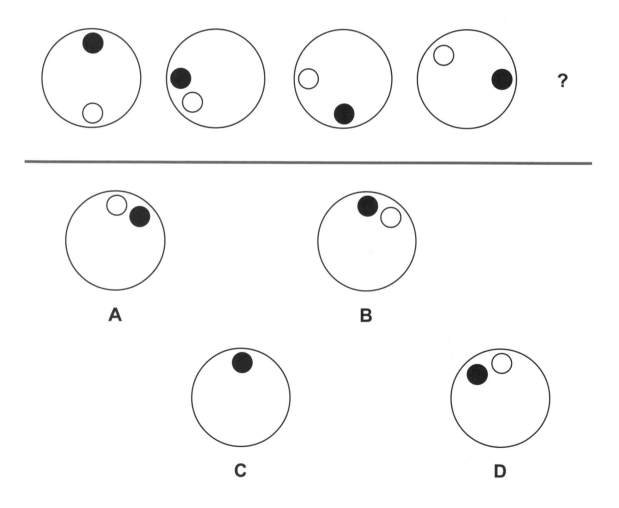

A   B

C   D

Creative Thinking and Co-ordination

Co-ordinate your hand to produce a mirror image of what your eyes see.

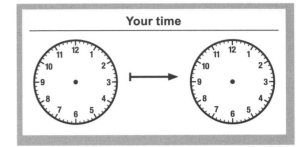

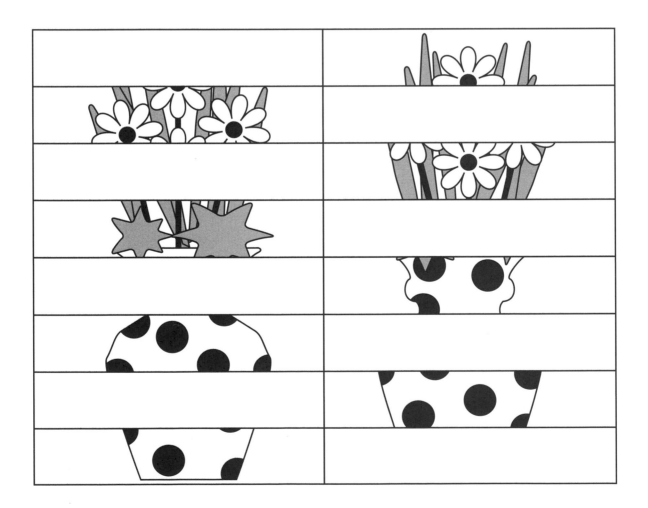

Memory

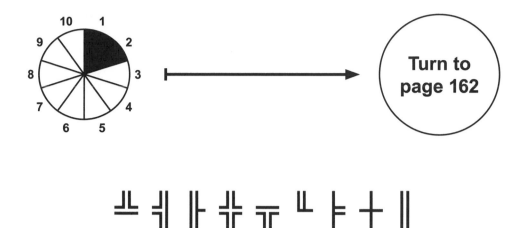

Turn to
page 162

Memory

Puzzle 119

Which of these did you see?

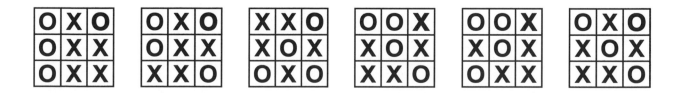

Tile Twister

Place the eight tiles into the grid so that all adjacent numbers on each tile match up. Any tile may be rotated, but no tile may be flipped over.

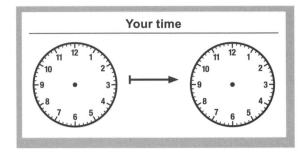

Your time

1	2
1	3

2	1
2	3

4	1
1	2

1	4
2	3

1	2
3	1

4	2
2	3

2	2
3	4

2	1
2	1

		2	2		
		2	2		

L-Shaped

Three pieces of each of the four kinds of shape shown below need to be inserted into the grid. Any piece may be turned or flipped over before being put in the grid. No pieces of the same kind can touch, even at a corner. Can you mark in where the Ls are?

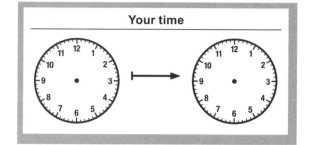

Your time

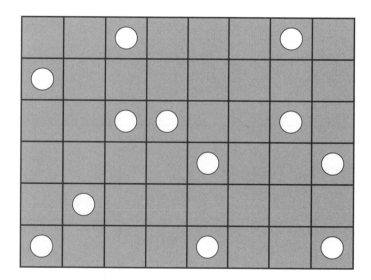

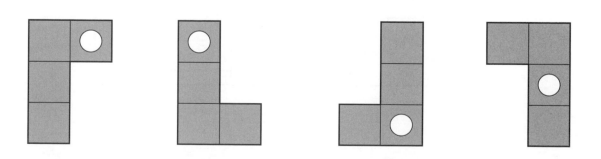

Progressive Matrix

Draw the contents of the missing tile in accordance with the rules of logic already established.

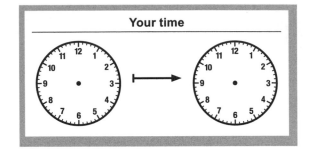

Your time

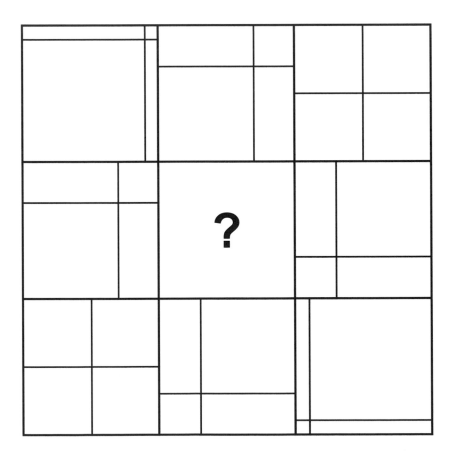

Odd One Out

Study the shapes carefully. Which is the odd one out?

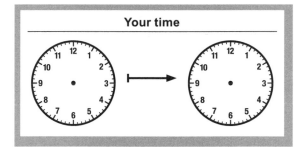

Your time

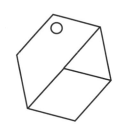

A

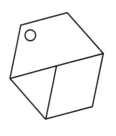

B

C

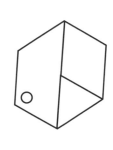

D

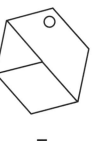

E

In Sequence

Study the sequence carefully. Which of the alternatives should take the place of the question mark?

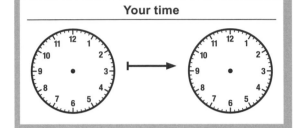

Your time

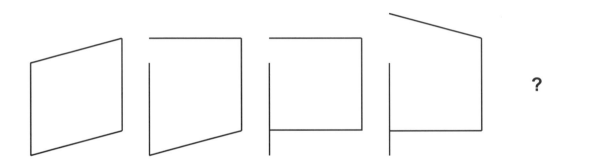

?

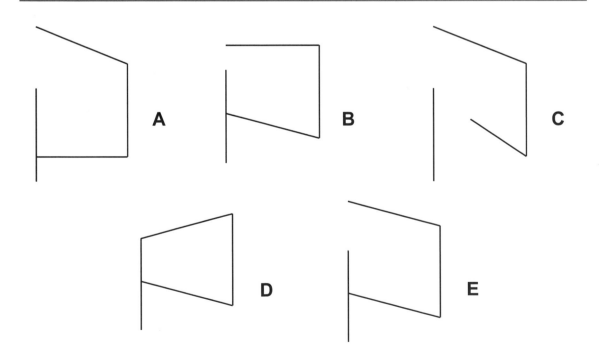

A

B

C

D

E

Folding Cubes

When the shape below is folded to form a cube, which is the only one of the following that can be produced?

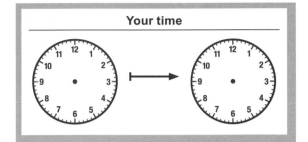

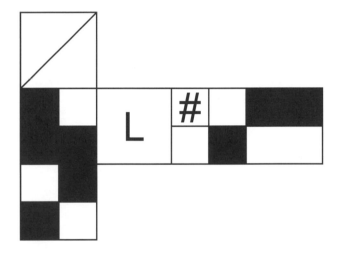

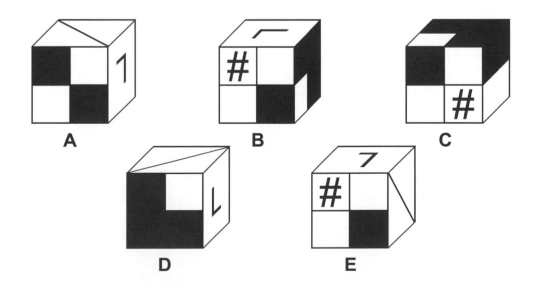

A   B   C

D   E

Memory

Turn to page 22

5 6 1 0 9 6 4 9 8

6 2 4 6 4 9 5 9

Memory

Puzzle 133

Which two symbols have changed places?

±	#	€
ß	¥	Œ
§	m	+

Tile Twister

Place the eight tiles into the grid so that all adjacent numbers on each tile match up. Any tile may be rotated, but no tile may be flipped over.

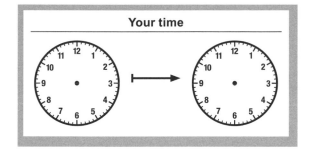

3	4
2	2

3	2
2	3

3	3
4	2

1	2
3	2

3	4
2	1

1	3
4	4

4	3
4	2

1	3
2	3

		3	4		
		2	3		

L-Shaped

Three pieces of each of the four kinds of shape shown below need to be inserted into the grid. Any piece may be turned or flipped over before being put in the grid. No pieces of the same kind can touch, even at a corner. Can you mark in where the Ls are?

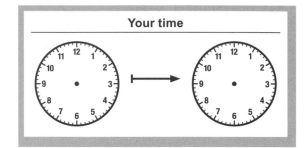

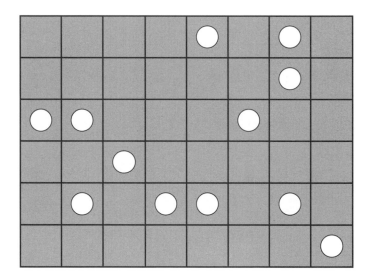

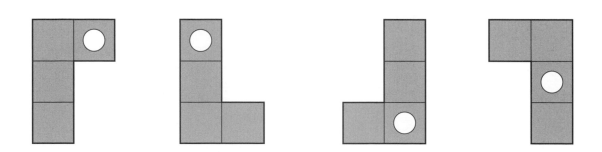

Progressive Matrix

Draw the contents of the missing tile
in accordance with the rules of logic
already established.

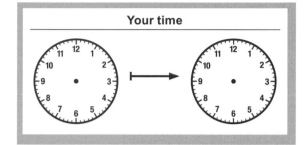

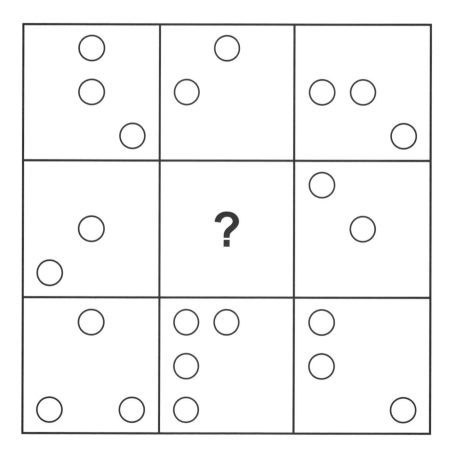

Odd One Out

Study the shapes carefully. Which is the odd one out?

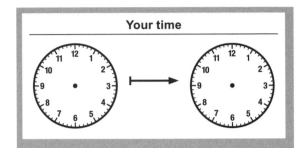

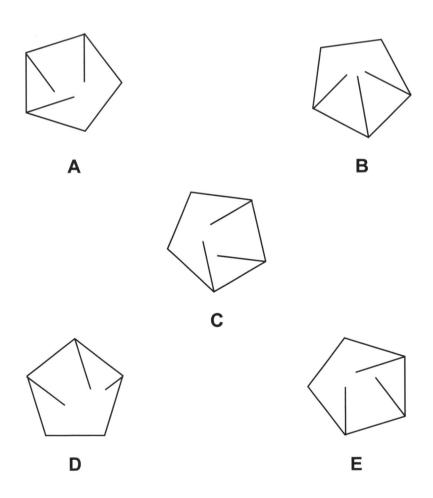

A

B

C

D

E

In Sequence

Study the sequence carefully. Which of the alternatives should take the place of the question mark?

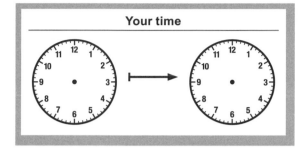

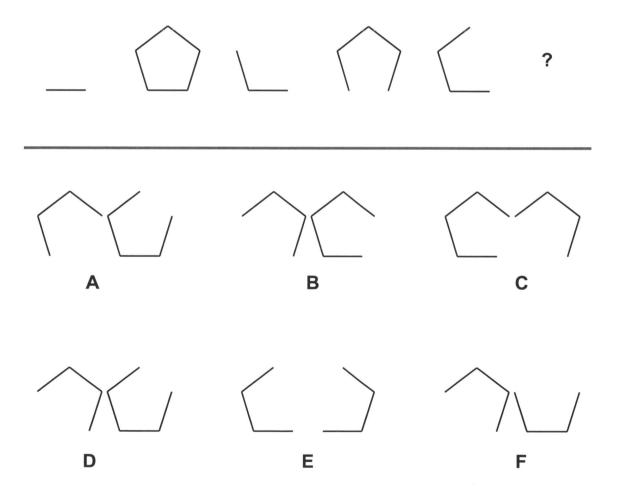

Folding Cubes

When the shape below is folded to form a cube, which is the only one of the following that can be produced?

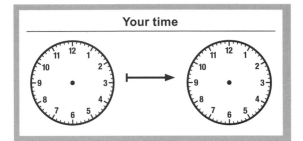

Your time

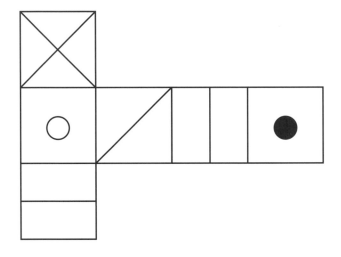

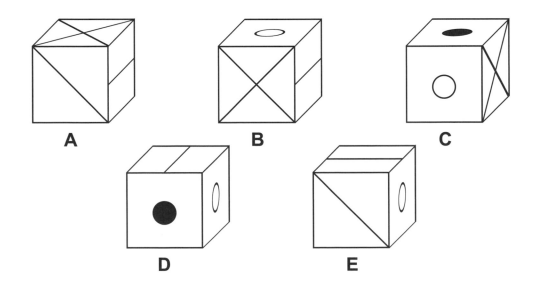

A   B   C

D   E

Memory

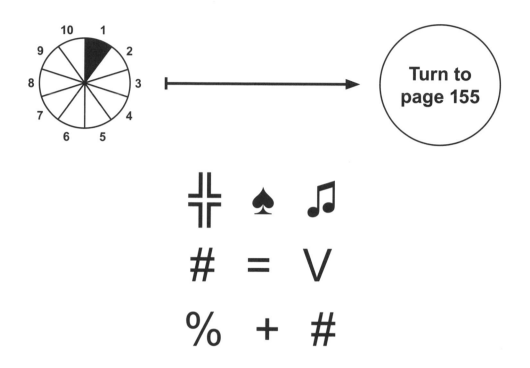

Turn to
page 155

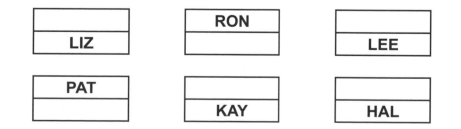

Memory

Puzzle 161

Put these into their correct positions:

BOB   EVE   PAM   KEN   JOE   SAM

	RON	
LIZ		LEE

PAT		
	KAY	HAL

Tile Twister

Place the eight tiles into the grid so that all adjacent numbers on each tile match up. Any tile may be rotated, but no tile may be flipped over.

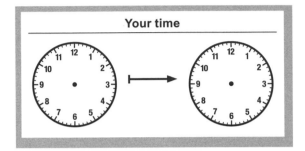

Your time

3	3
4	2

2	3
4	4

4	3
1	3

3	4
2	1

4	3
1	4

1	3
2	3

4	3
3	2

1	2
1	3

L-Shaped

Three pieces of each of the four kinds of shape shown below need to be inserted into the grid. Any piece may be turned or flipped over before being put in the grid. No pieces of the same kind can touch, even at a corner. Can you mark in where the Ls are?

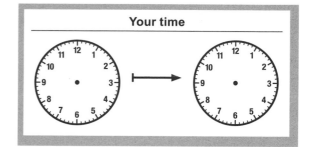

Your time

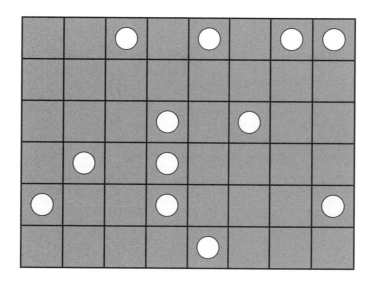

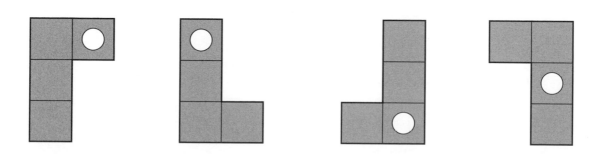

Progressive Matrix

Draw the contents of the missing tile in accordance with the rules of logic already established.

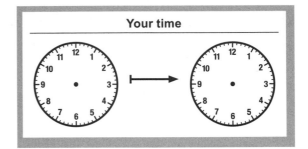

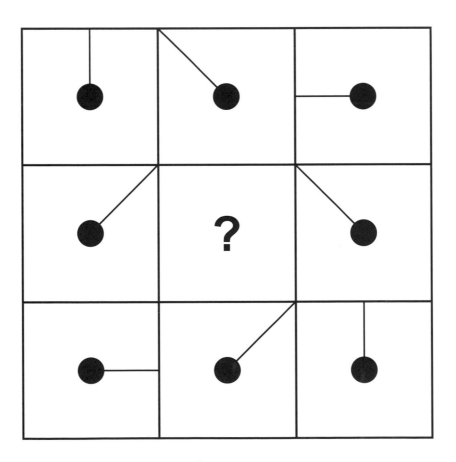

Odd One Out

Study the shapes carefully. Which is the odd one out?

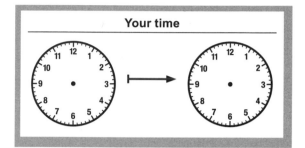

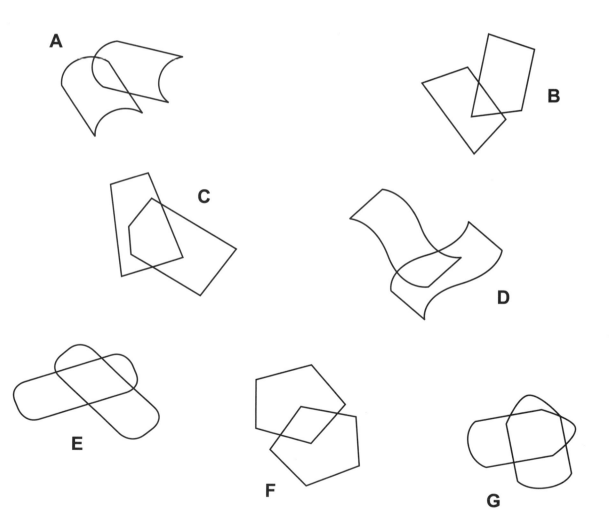

A

B

C

D

E

F

G

In Sequence

Study the sequence carefully. Which of the alternatives should take the place of the question mark?

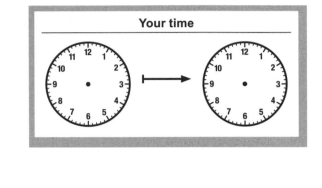

Your time

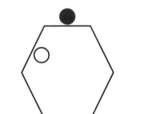 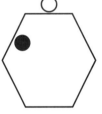 **?**

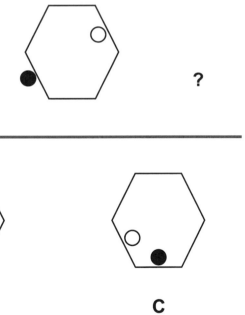

A

B

C

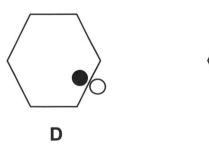

D

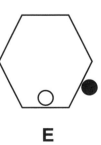

E

Creative Thinking and Co-ordination

Co-ordinate your hand to produce a mirror image of what your eyes see.

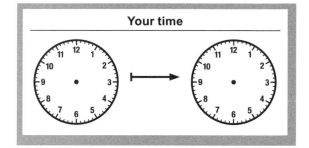

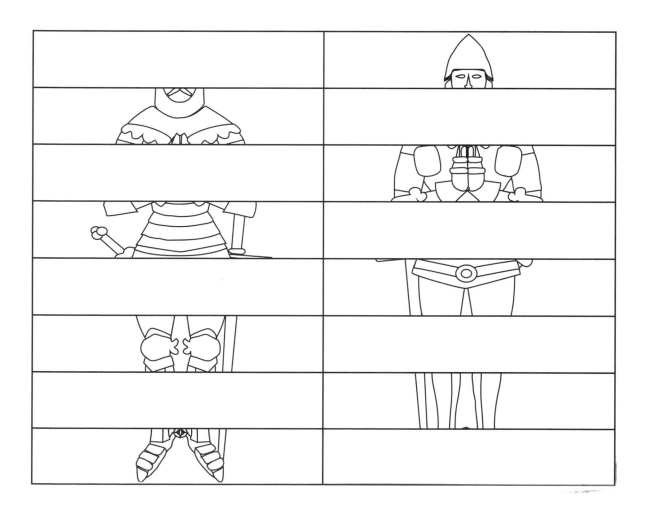

Memory

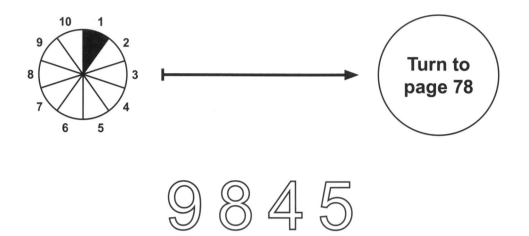

Turn to page 78

9845

Memory

Puzzle 147

Which of the following is a list of the second, third and sixth letters in that order?

R L J	P L J
R P U	R P J
R L U	P L U

Tile Twister

Place the eight tiles into the grid so that all adjacent numbers on each tile match up. Any tile may be rotated, but no tile may be flipped over.

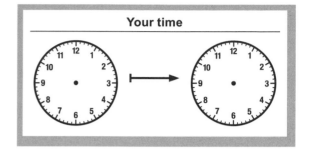

4	2
3	4

3	3
1	3

4	2
1	3

1	4
2	3

3	4
2	2

1	2
1	4

1	3
4	2

3	1
4	3

2	2			
3	3			

L-Shaped

Three pieces of each of the four kinds of shape shown below need to be inserted into the grid. Any piece may be turned or flipped over before being put in the grid. No pieces of the same kind can touch, even at a corner. Can you mark in where the Ls are?

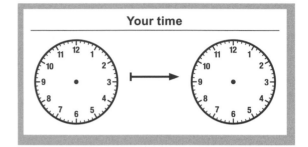

Your time

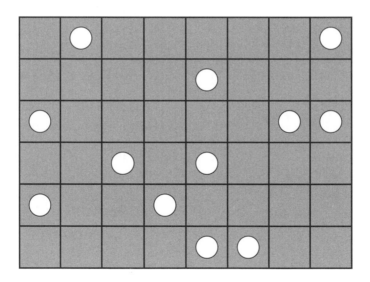

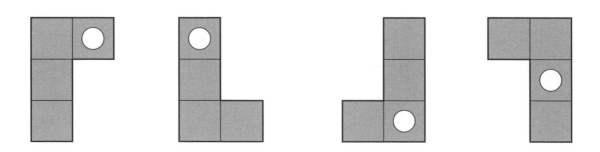

Progressive Matrix

Draw the contents of the missing tile in accordance with the rules of logic already established.

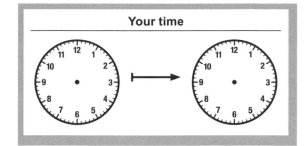

Your time

B	E	H
F	K	P
J	Q	?

Odd One Out

Study the shapes carefully. Which is the odd one out?

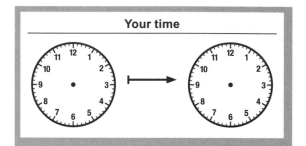

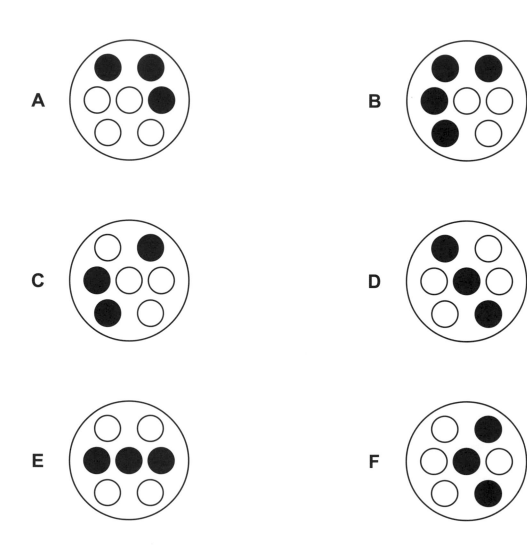

A

B

C

D

E

F

In Sequence

Study the sequence carefully. Which of the alternatives should take the place of the question mark?

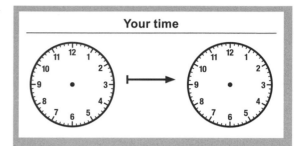

 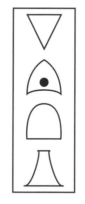 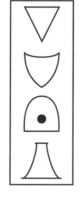

?

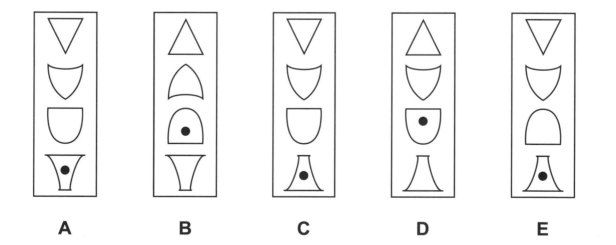

A **B** **C** **D** **E**

Folding Cubes

When the shape below is folded to form a cube, which is the only one of the following that can be produced?

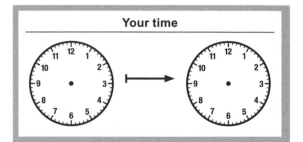

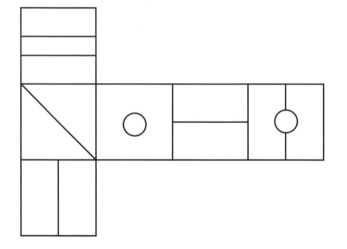

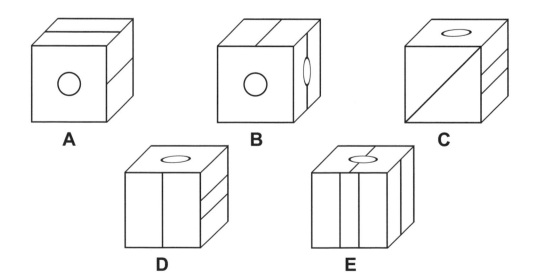

A   B   C

D   E

Memory

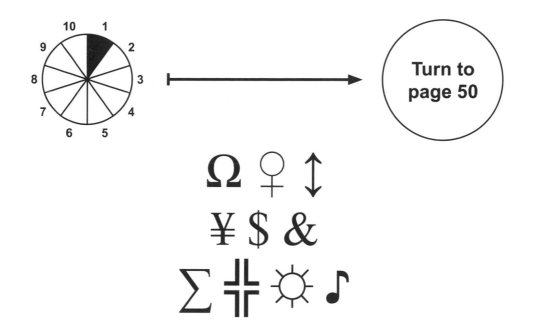

Turn to page 50

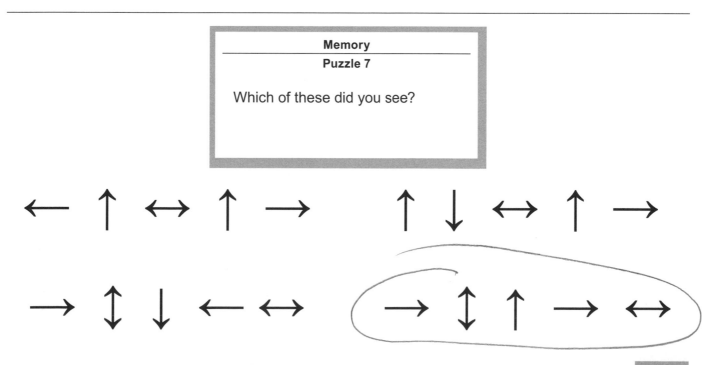

Memory

Puzzle 7

Which of these did you see?

Tile Twister

Place the eight tiles into the grid so that all adjacent numbers on each tile match up. Any tile may be rotated, but no tile may be flipped over.

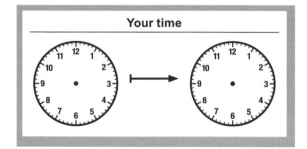

Your time

3	1
2	1

2	2
1	2

3	1
3	2

4	4
3	2

2	2
3	4

4	2
1	1

2	1
4	2

2	4
4	1

				2	1
				2	3

L-Shaped

Three pieces of each of the four kinds of shape shown below need to be inserted into the grid. Any piece may be turned or flipped over before being put in the grid. No pieces of the same kind can touch, even at a corner. Can you mark in where the Ls are?

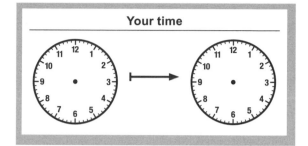

Your time

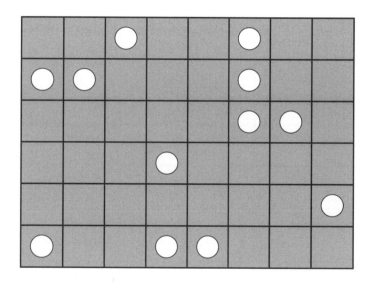

Progressive Matrix

Draw the contents of the missing tile in accordance with the rules of logic already established.

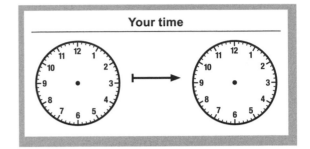

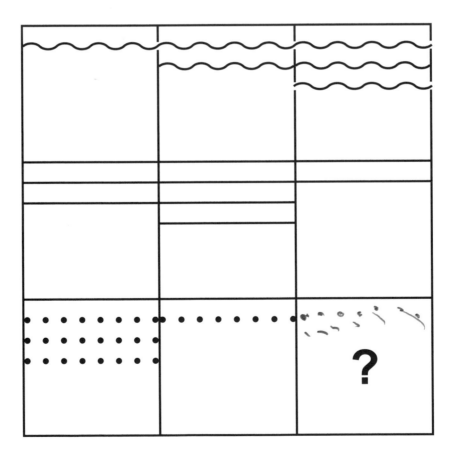

Odd One Out

Study the shapes carefully. Which is the odd one out?

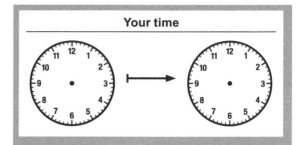

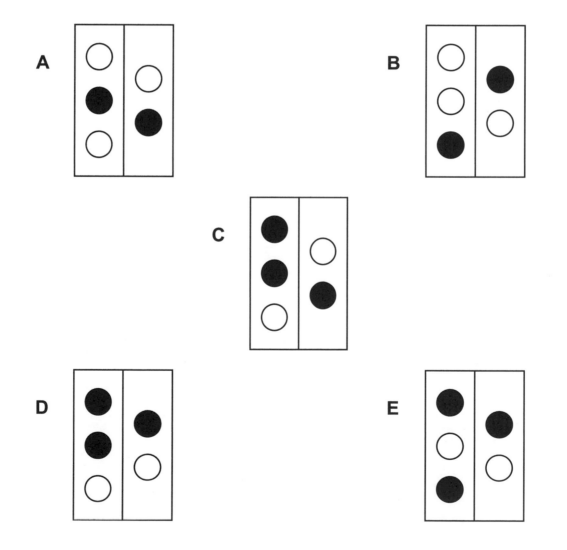

In Sequence

Study the sequence carefully. Which of the alternatives should take the place of the question mark?

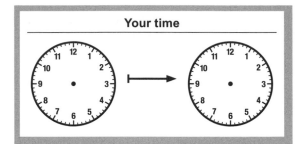

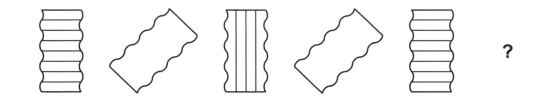

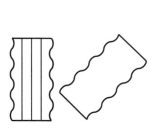

A

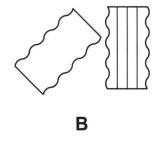

B

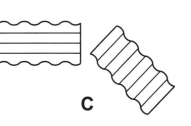

C

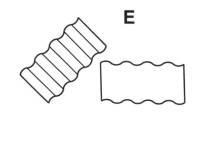

D

E

F

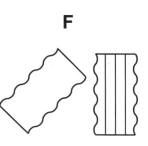

Folding Cubes

When the shape below is folded to form a cube, which is the only one of the following that can be produced?

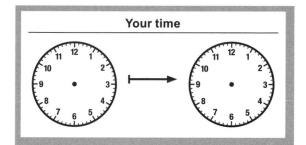

Your time

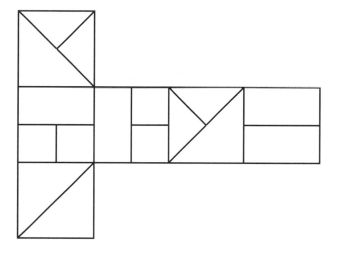

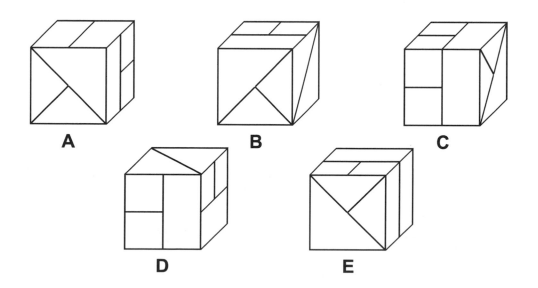

A   B   C

D   E

Memory

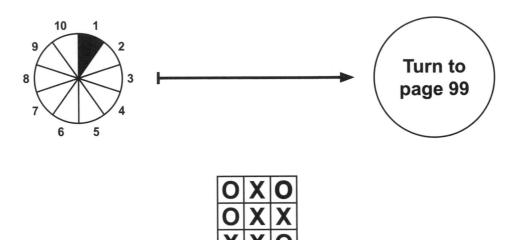

Turn to
page 99

O	X	O
O	X	X
X	X	O

Memory

Puzzle 70

Which of these did you see?

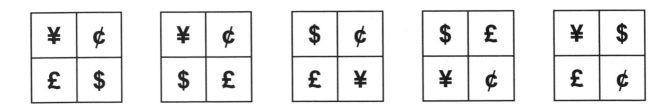

Tile Twister

Place the eight tiles into the grid so that all adjacent numbers on each tile match up. Any tile may be rotated, but no tile may be flipped over.

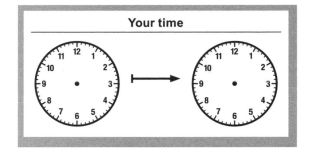

Your time

3	1
4	4

3	1
2	2

1	3
1	2

4	1
2	2

4	2
4	3

3	3
1	2

3	3
1	1

3	2
1	3

		1	2		
		2	2		

L-Shaped

Three pieces of each of the four kinds of shape shown below need to be inserted into the grid. Any piece may be turned or flipped over before being put in the grid. No pieces of the same kind can touch, even at a corner. Can you mark in where the Ls are?

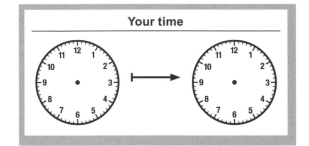

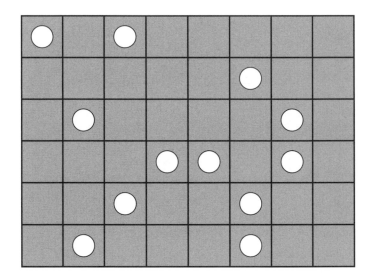

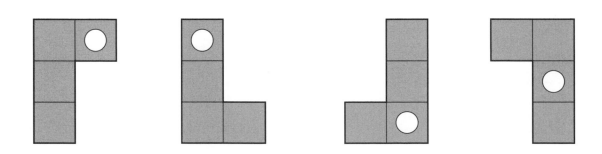

Progressive Matrix

Draw the contents of the missing tile
in accordance with the rules of logic
already established.

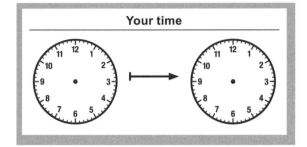

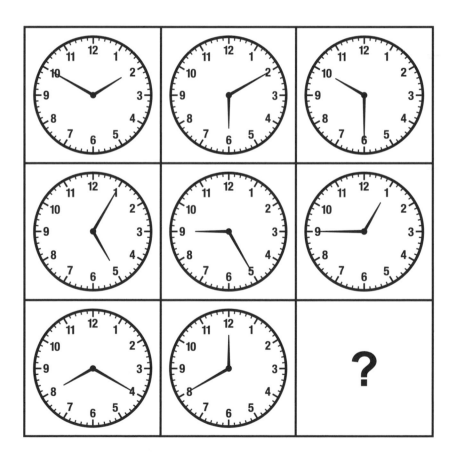

Odd One Out

Study the shapes carefully. Which is the odd one out?

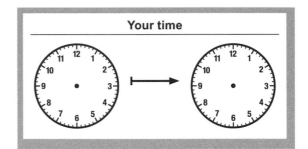
Your time

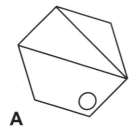

A

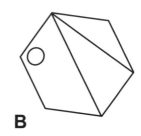

B

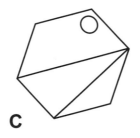

C

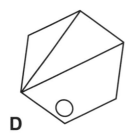

D

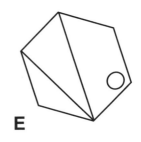

E

In Sequence

Study the sequence carefully. Which of the alternatives should take the place of the question mark?

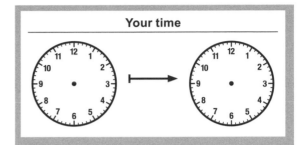

Your time

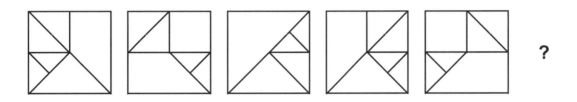

?

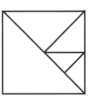

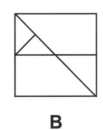

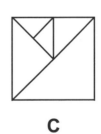

A

B

C

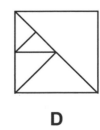

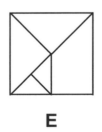

D

E

Creative Thinking and Co-ordination

Co-ordinate your hand to produce a mirror image of what your eyes see.

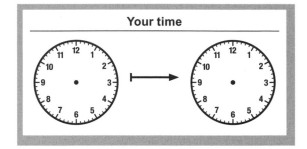

Memory

Turn to page 29

A D L C T N V
R P S V L J R
D F O J F W E

Memory

Puzzle 28

Which new symbol has appeared?
Which two have changed places?
Which has been removed?

Tile Twister

Place the eight tiles into the grid so that all adjacent numbers on each tile match up. Any tile may be rotated, but no tile may be flipped over.

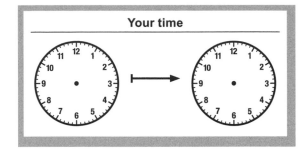

Your time

4	2
4	1

2	4
3	3

3	2
2	3

3	1
2	2

2	3
1	4

4	1
3	4

4	1
4	4

1	3
3	4

		1	1		
		3	3		

L-Shaped

Three pieces of each of the four kinds of shape shown below need to be inserted into the grid. Any piece may be turned or flipped over before being put in the grid. No pieces of the same kind can touch, even at a corner. Can you mark in where the Ls are?

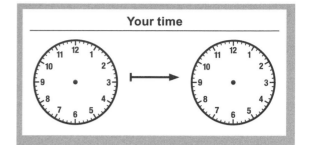

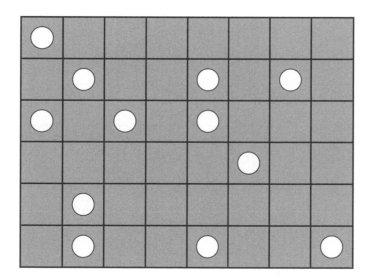

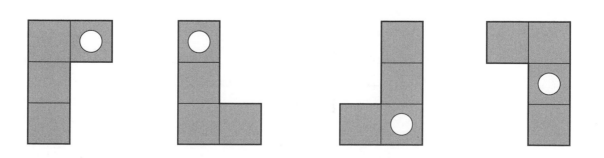

Progressive Matrix

Draw the contents of the missing tile in accordance with the rules of logic already established.

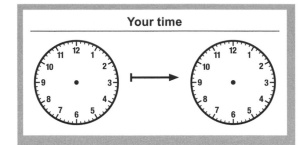

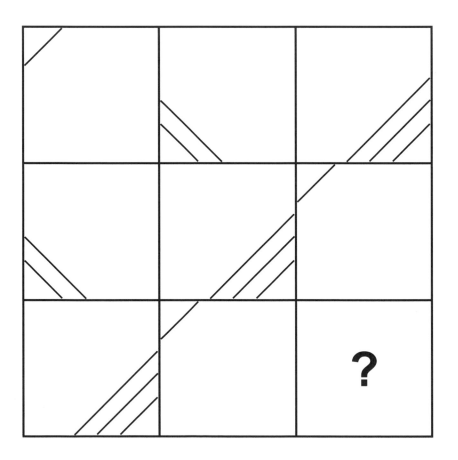

Odd One Out

Study the shapes carefully. Which is the odd one out?

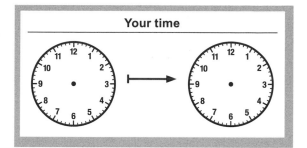

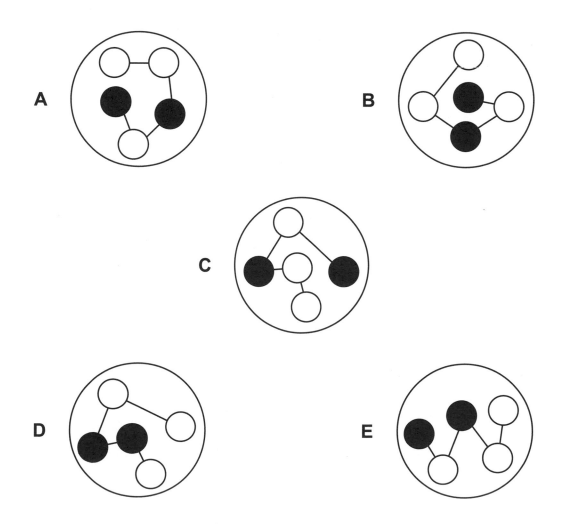

A

B

C

D

E

In Sequence

Study the sequence carefully. Which of the alternatives should take the place of the question mark?

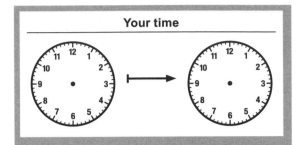

Your time

?

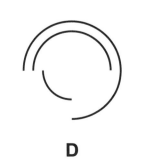

A

B

C

D

E

Folding Cubes

When the shape below is folded to form a cube, which is the only one of the following that can be produced?

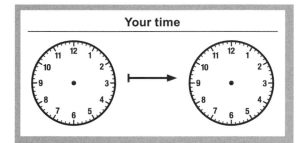

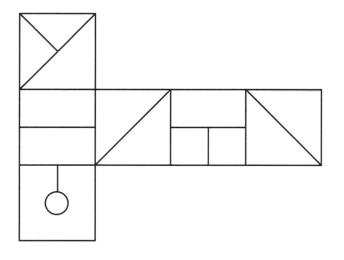

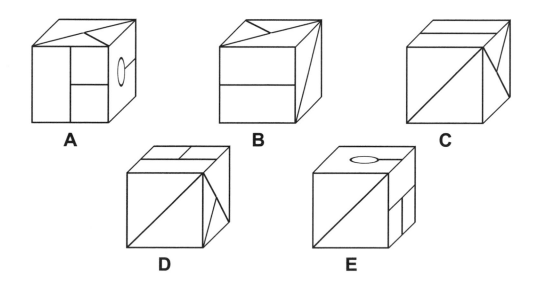

Memory

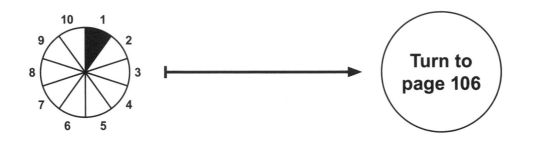

Turn to page 106

±	#	¥
ß	€	Œ
§	m	+

Memory

Puzzle 49

Which of the following three numbers occurs more than once in the sequence?

364   976

953   164   497

Tile Twister

Place the eight tiles into the grid so that all adjacent numbers on each tile match up. Any tile may be rotated, but no tile may be flipped over.

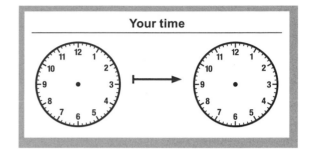

Your time

2	3
2	2

1	4
3	2

1	2
1	2

2	1
4	3

1	2
4	4

2	4
3	3

3	2
2	1

2	3
2	1

				3	4
				3	1

L-Shaped

Three pieces of each of the four kinds of shape shown below need to be inserted into the grid. Any piece may be turned or flipped over before being put in the grid. No pieces of the same kind can touch, even at a corner. Can you mark in where the Ls are?

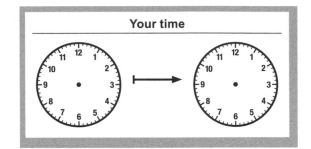

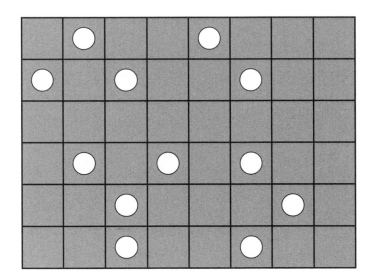

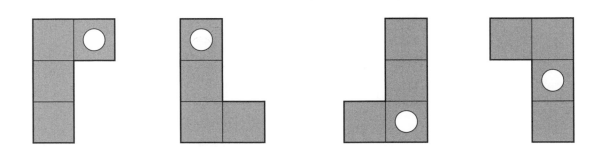

Progressive Matrix

Draw the contents of the missing tile in accordance with the rules of logic already established.

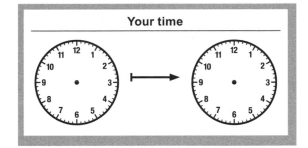

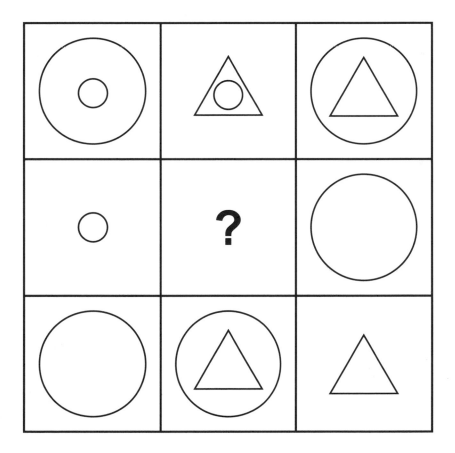

Odd One Out

Study the shapes carefully. Which is the odd one out?

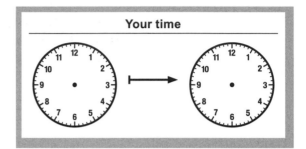

Your time

A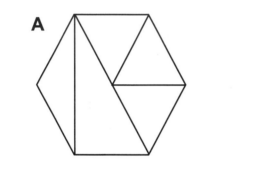

B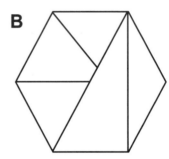

C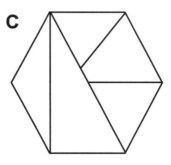

D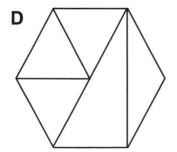

E

In Sequence

Study the sequence carefully. Which of
the alternatives should take the place
of the question mark?

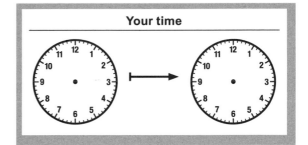

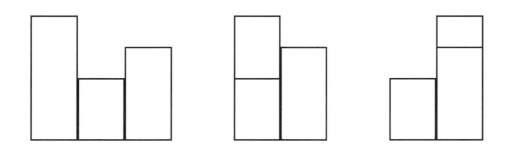

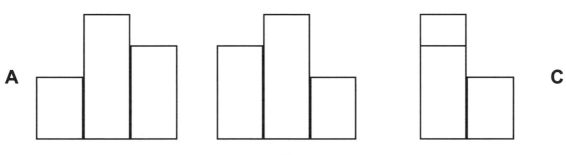

A

B

C

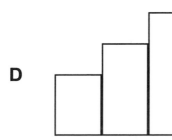

D

E

Folding Cubes

When the shape below is folded to form a cube, which is the only one of the following that can be produced?

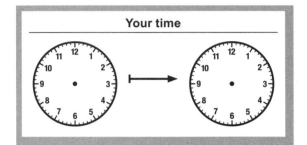

Your time

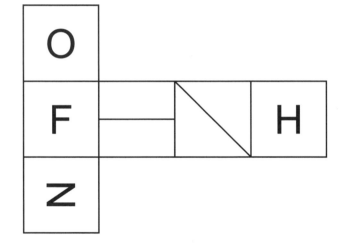

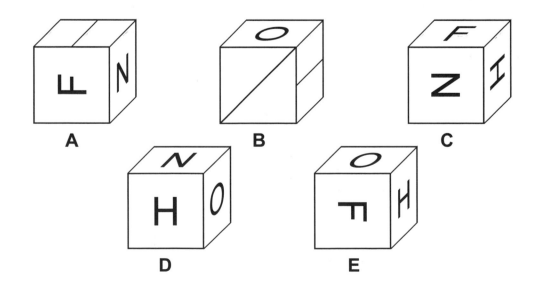

A

B

C

D

E

Memory

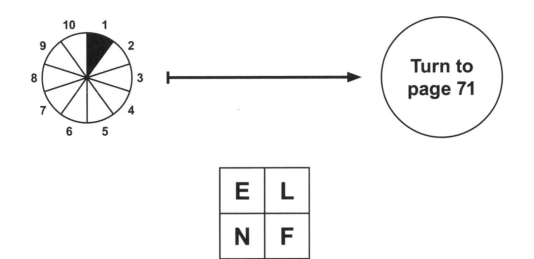

Turn to
page 71

E	L
N	F

Memory

Puzzle 98

Answer the questions below.

Which is the only letter that appears in the list?

Which is the only symbol to appear twice in the list?

Which is the penultimate symbol listed?

Tile Twister

Place the eight tiles into the grid so that all adjacent numbers on each tile match up. Any tile may be rotated, but no tile may be flipped over.

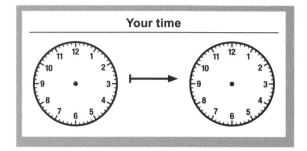

Your time

2	4
4	1

3	4
4	2

1	2
4	3

4	4
1	3

1	2
1	4

4	3
1	4

4	2
4	1

1	4
3	1

2	3				
4	4				

L-Shaped

Three pieces of each of the four kinds of shape shown below need to be inserted into the grid. Any piece may be turned or flipped over before being put in the grid. No pieces of the same kind can touch, even at a corner. Can you mark in where the Ls are?

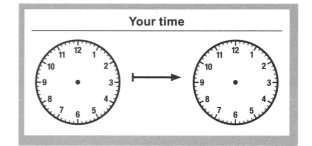

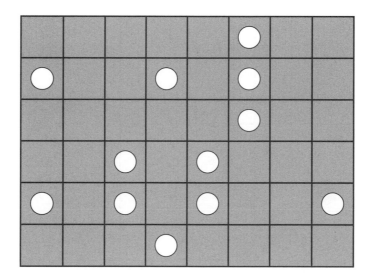

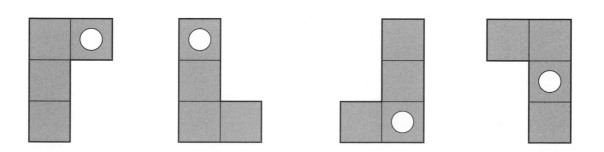

Progressive Matrix

Draw the contents of the missing tile
in accordance with the rules of logic
already established.

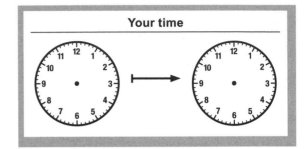

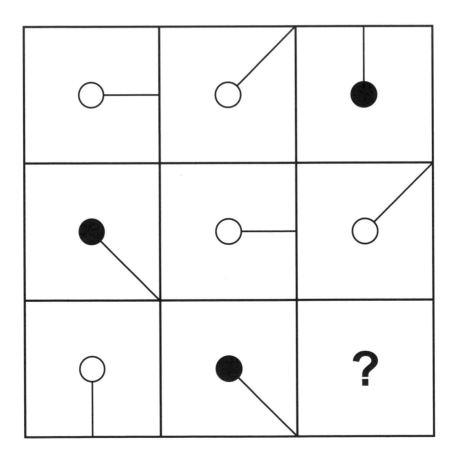

Odd One Out

Study the shapes carefully. Which is the odd one out?

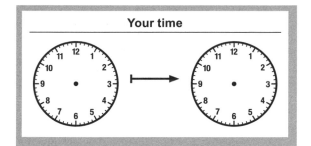

Your time

A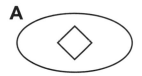

B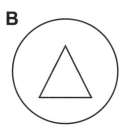

C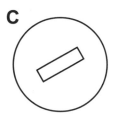

D

E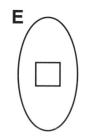

F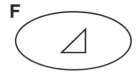

In Sequence

Study the sequence carefully. Which of the alternatives should take the place of the question mark?

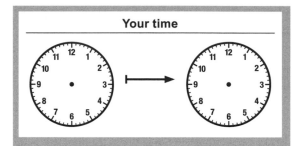

Your time

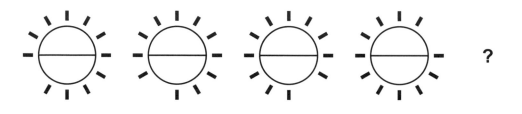 ?

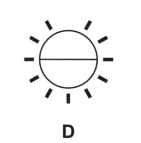

A

B

C

D

E

Creative Thinking and Co-ordination

Co-ordinate your hand to produce a mirror image of what your eyes see.

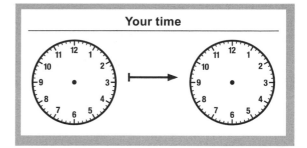

Memory

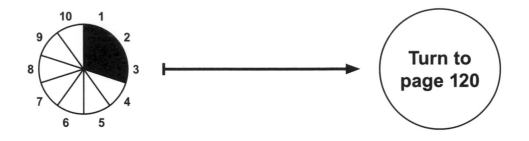

Turn to page 120

A R P L U J N

Memory

Puzzle 84

Which TWO of these groups of three symbols appear in the same order next to each other?

Tile Twister

Place the eight tiles into the grid so that all adjacent numbers on each tile match up. Any tile may be rotated, but no tile may be flipped over.

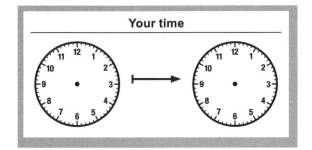

Your time

1	2
3	3

3	3
2	4

1	3
1	4

2	4
1	1

3	2
1	1

2	1
4	2

4	2
2	4

4	4
1	2

2	4				
3	4				

L-Shaped

Three pieces of each of the four kinds of shape shown below need to be inserted into the grid. Any piece may be turned or flipped over before being put in the grid. No pieces of the same kind can touch, even at a corner. Can you mark in where the Ls are?

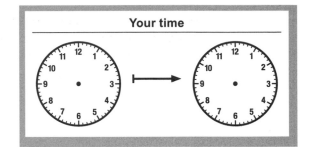

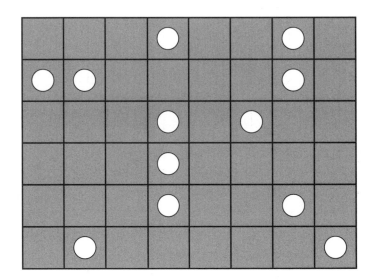

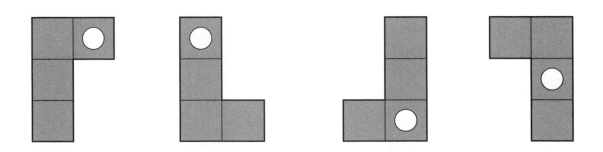

Progressive Matrix

Draw the contents of the missing tile in accordance with the rules of logic already established.

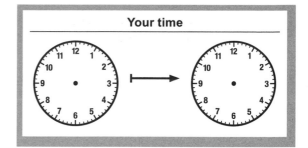

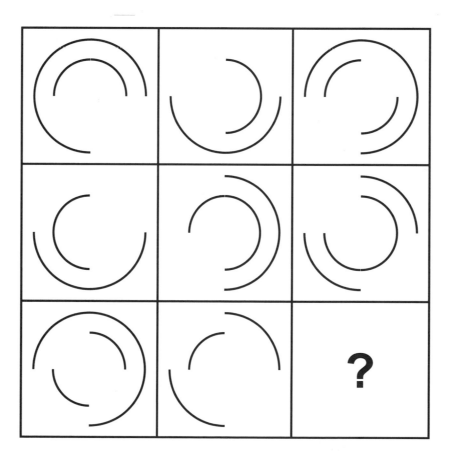

Odd One Out

Study the shapes carefully. Which is the odd one out?

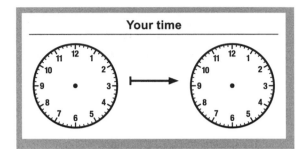

Your time

A

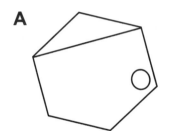

B

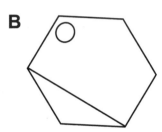

C

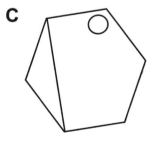

D

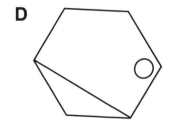

E

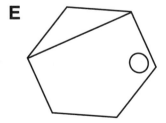

In Sequence

Study the sequence carefully. Which of the alternatives should take the place of the question mark?

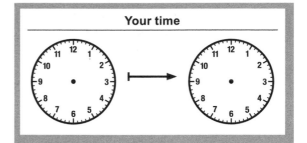

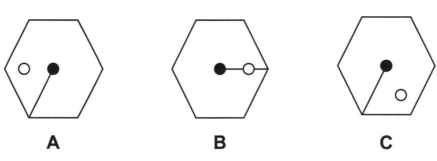

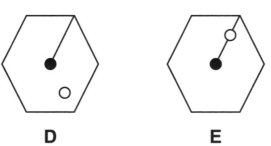

Folding Cubes

When the shape below is folded to form a cube, which is the only one of the following that can be produced?

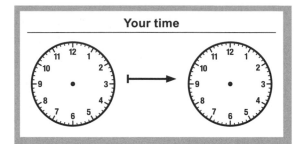

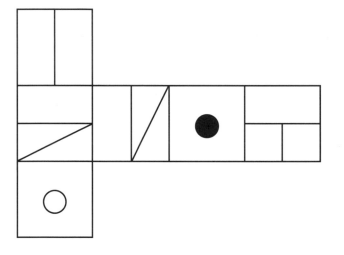

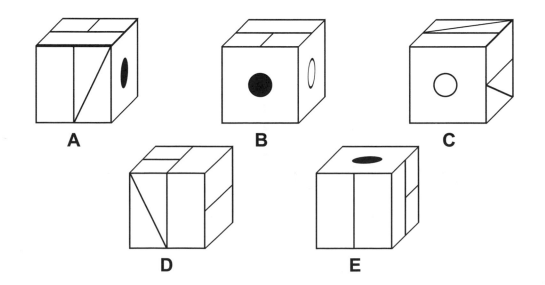

A   B   C

D   E

Memory

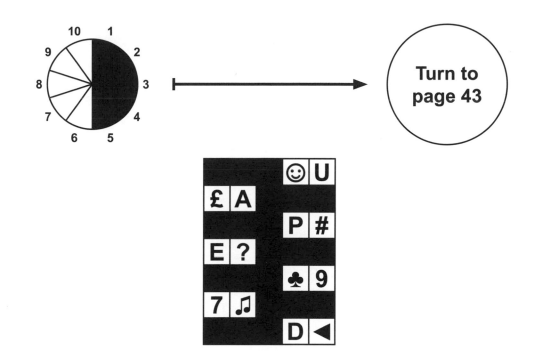

Turn to page 43

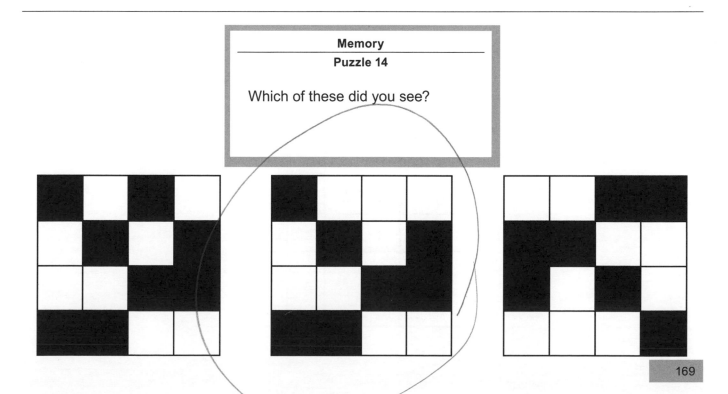

Memory

Puzzle 14

Which of these did you see?

Tile Twister

Place the eight tiles into the grid so that all adjacent numbers on each tile match up. Any tile may be rotated, but no tile may be flipped over.

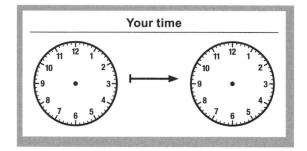

Your time

3	2
2	4

1	3
3	2

4	3
2	2

3	4
1	3

3	1
2	1

3	4
2	2

1	1
2	4

3	4
2	3

L-Shaped

Three pieces of each of the four kinds of shape shown below need to be inserted into the grid. Any piece may be turned or flipped over before being put in the grid. No pieces of the same kind can touch, even at a corner. Can you mark in where the Ls are?

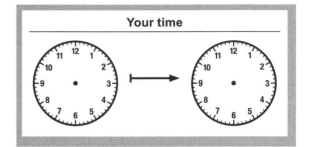

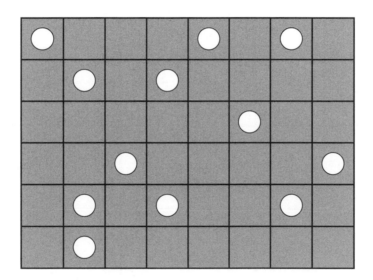

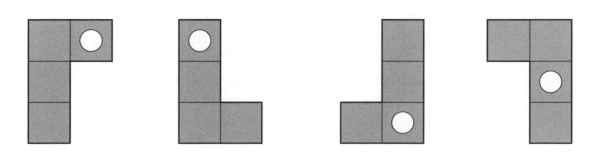

Progressive Matrix

Draw the contents of the missing tile in accordance with the rules of logic already established.

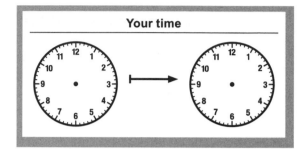

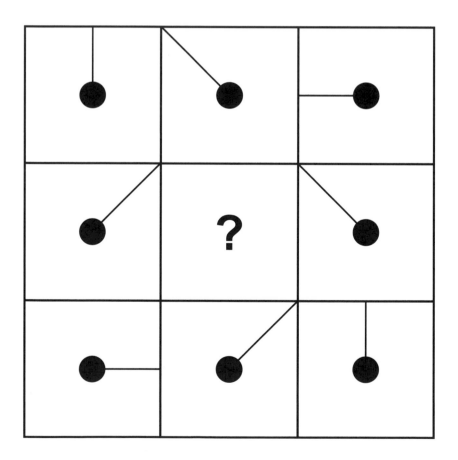

Odd One Out

Study the shapes carefully. Which is the odd one out?

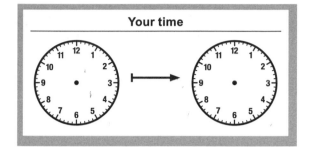
Your time

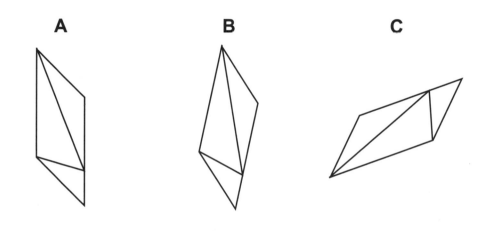

A   B   C

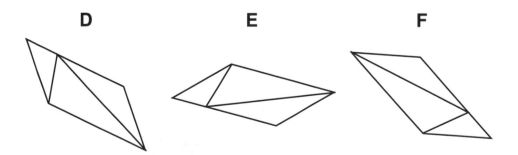

D   E   F

In Sequence

Study the sequence carefully. Which of the alternatives should take the place of the question mark?

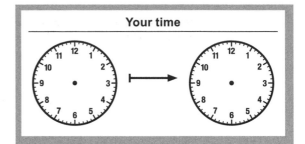

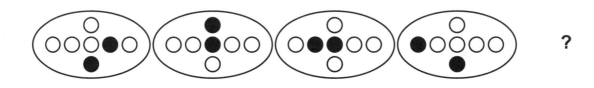

?

A

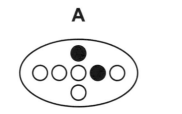

B

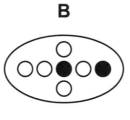

C

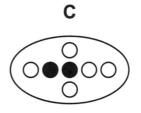

D

E

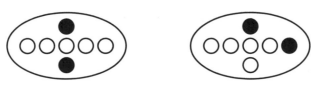

Folding Cubes

When the shape below is folded to form a cube, which is the only one of the following that can be produced?

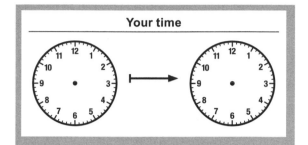

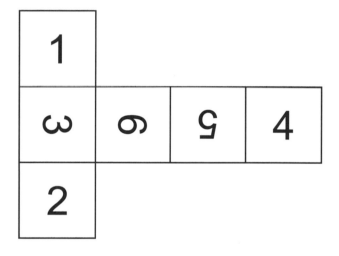

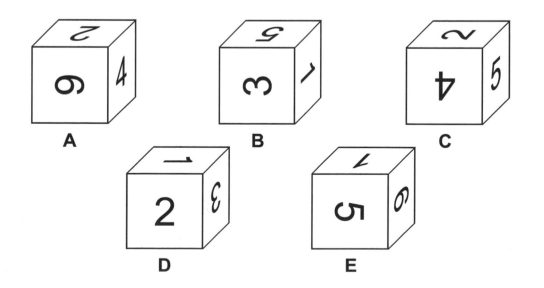

Memory

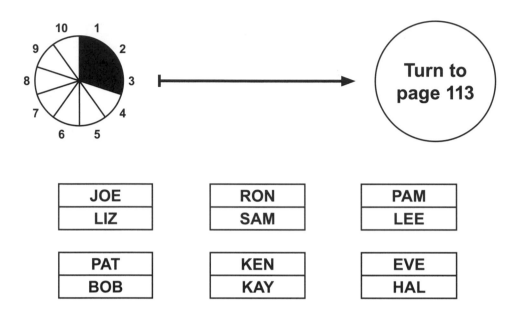

Turn to page 113

JOE		RON		PAM
LIZ		SAM		LEE

PAT		KEN		EVE
BOB		KAY		HAL

Memory

Puzzle 42

Which of these did you see?

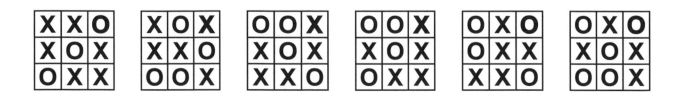

Tile Twister

Place the eight tiles into the grid so that all adjacent numbers on each tile match up. Any tile may be rotated, but no tile may be flipped over.

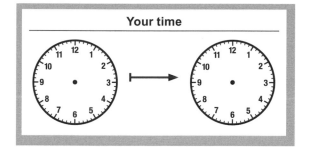

Your time

4	4
3	1

1	1
4	2

4	3
1	3

4	2
3	1

4	4
1	2

4	2
3	4

1	1
3	2

3	2
3	4

2	1				
2	1				

L-Shaped

Three pieces of each of the four kinds of shape shown below need to be inserted into the grid. Any piece may be turned or flipped over before being put in the grid. No pieces of the same kind can touch, even at a corner. Can you mark in where the Ls are?

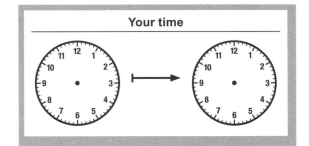

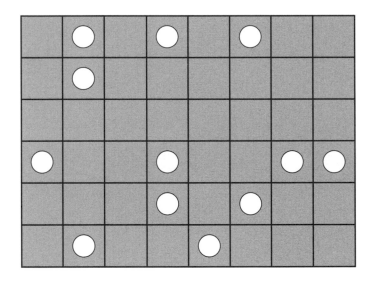

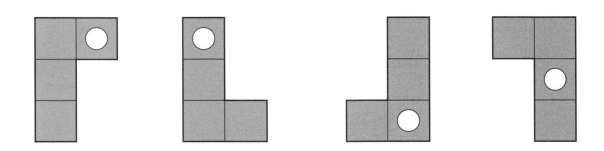

Progressive Matrix

Draw the contents of the missing tile in accordance with the rules of logic already established.

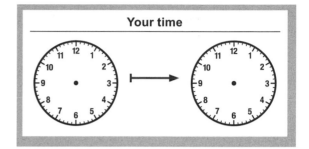

Your time

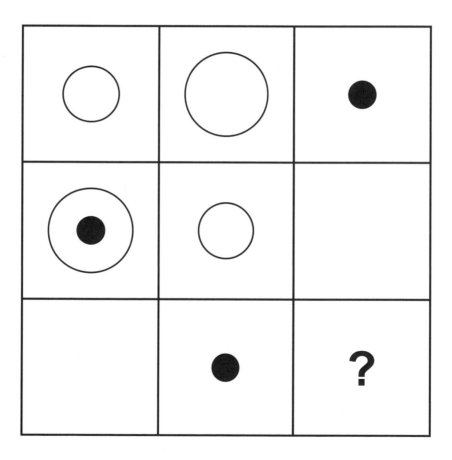

Odd One Out

Study the shapes carefully. Which is the odd one out?

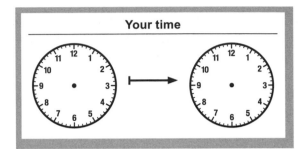

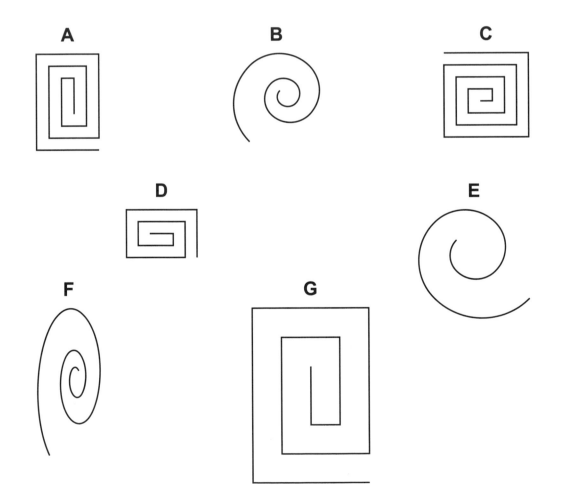

A

B

C

D

E

F

G

In Sequence

Study the sequence carefully. Which of the alternatives should take the place of the question mark?

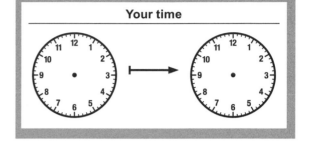

Your time

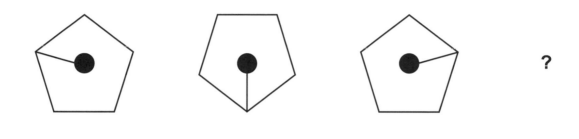

?

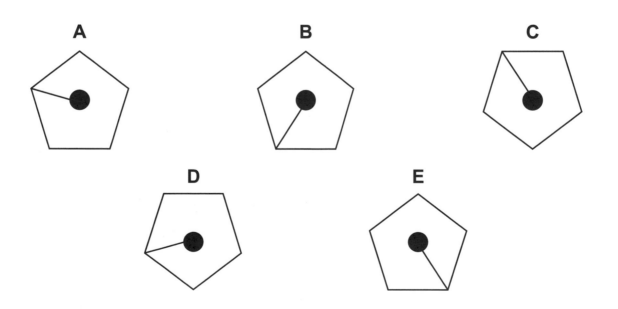

A

B

C

D

E

Creative Thinking and Co-ordination

Co-ordinate your hand to produce a
mirror image of what your eyes see.

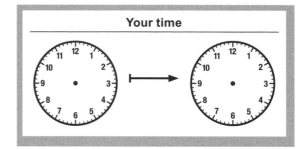

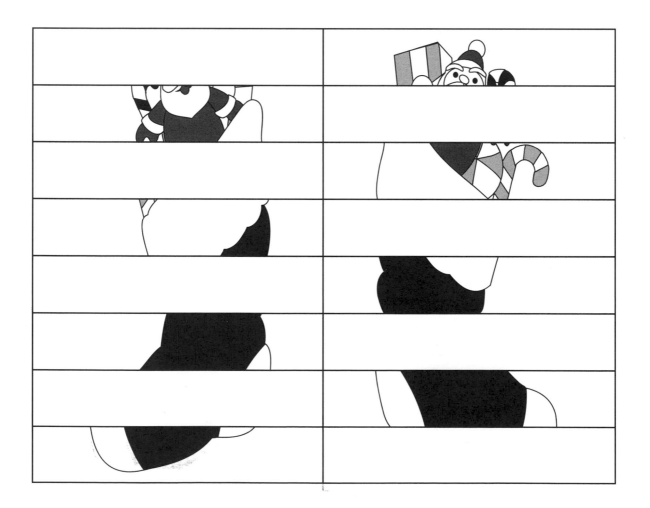

Memory

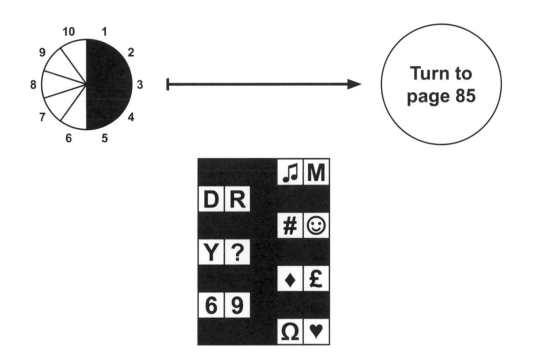

Turn to page 85

Memory

Puzzle 35

Answer the questions below.

What number ends the third row?

What number appears twice on the top row?

What number appears at the beginning and middle of the second row?

Tile Twister

Place the eight tiles into the grid so that all adjacent numbers on each tile match up. Any tile may be rotated, but no tile may be flipped over.

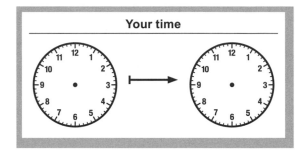

Your time

4	3
1	3

1	4
2	2

4	3
2	2

4	3
3	2

2	4
3	3

2	3
4	1

2	1
4	3

2	3
1	1

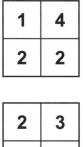

L-Shaped

Three pieces of each of the four kinds of shape shown below need to be inserted into the grid. Any piece may be turned or flipped over before being put in the grid. No pieces of the same kind can touch, even at a corner. Can you mark in where the Ls are?

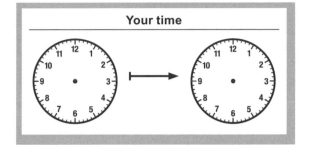

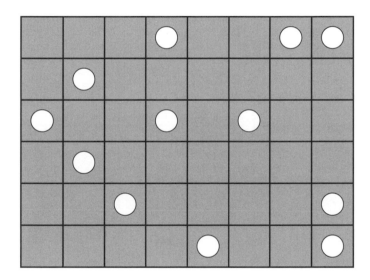

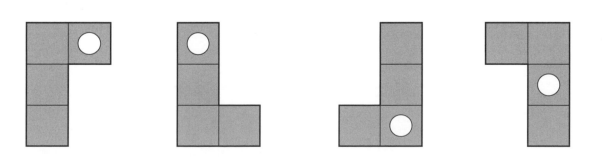

Progressive Matrix

Draw the contents of the missing tile
in accordance with the rules of logic
already established.

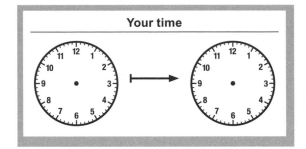

Odd One Out

Study the shapes carefully. Which is the odd one out?

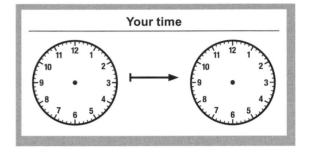

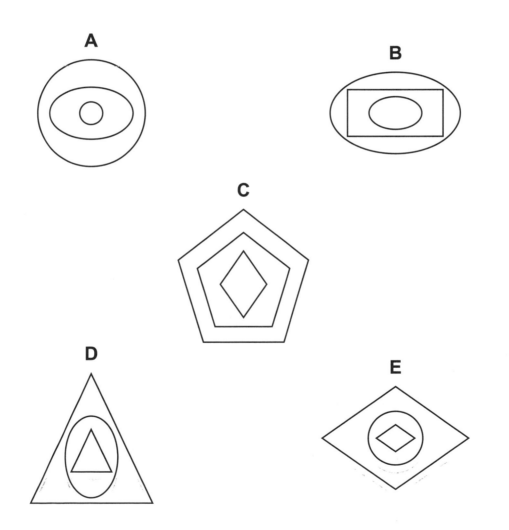

In Sequence

Study the sequence carefully. Which of the alternatives should take the place of the question mark?

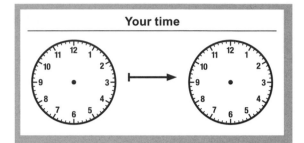

Your time

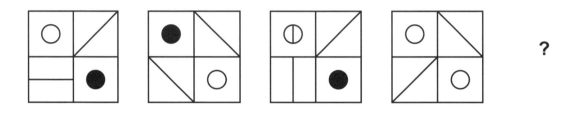

?

A

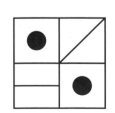

B

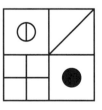

C

D

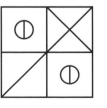

E

188

Folding Cubes

When the shape below is folded to form a cube, which is the only one of the following that can be produced?

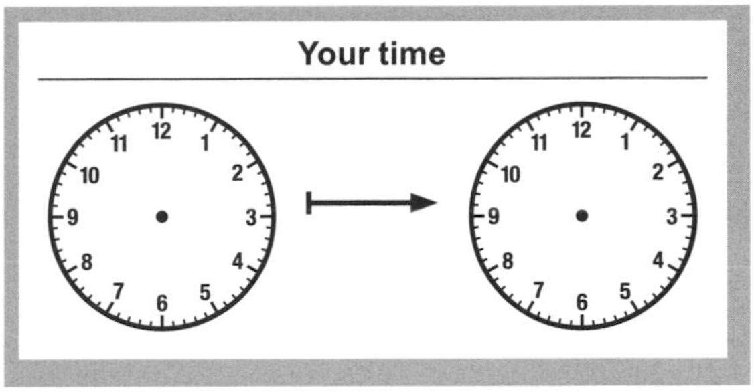

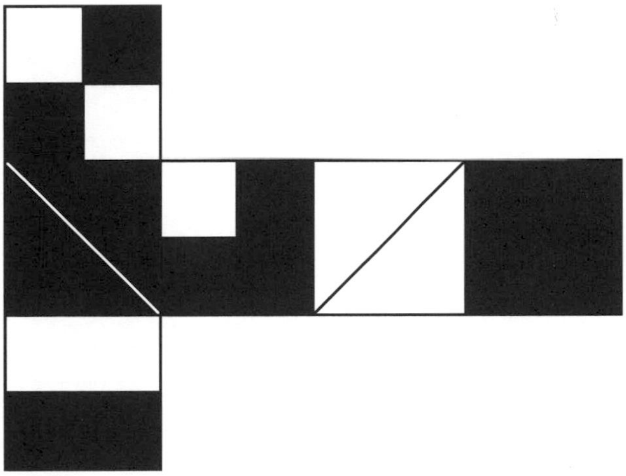

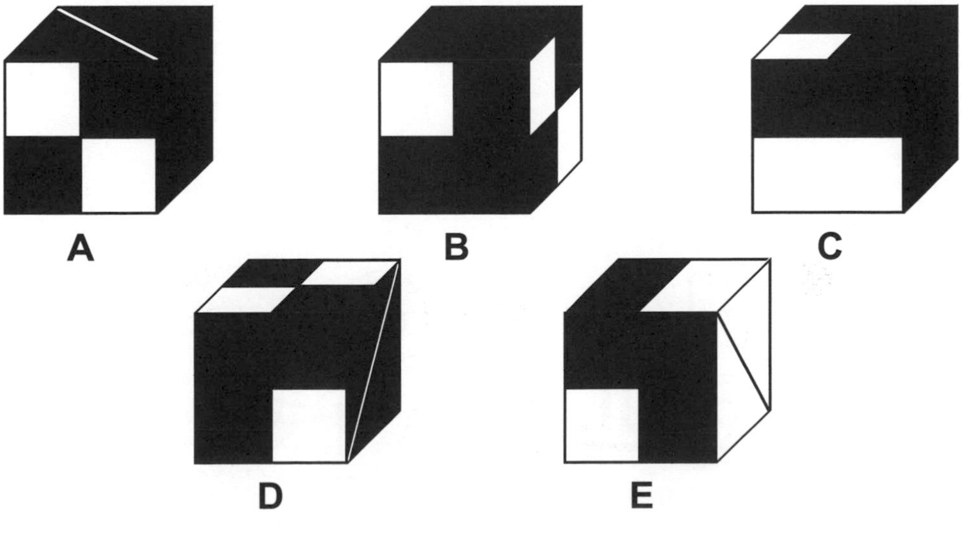

Your time

A

B

C

D

E

Memory

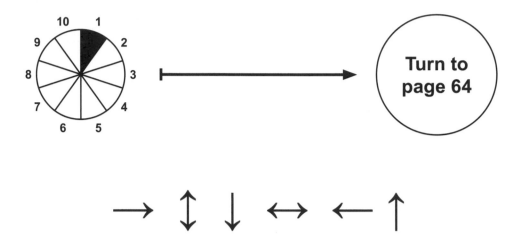

Turn to page 64

Memory

Puzzle 21

Which new symbol has been added?

Tile Twister

Place the eight tiles into the grid so that all adjacent numbers on each tile match up. Any tile may be rotated, but no tile may be flipped over.

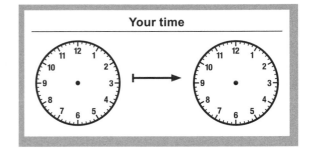

Your time

1	3
3	4

2	1
3	4

3	4
4	3

2	3
1	4

1	3
2	3

3	4
3	2

4	3
4	1

4	1
4	2

				2	2
				3	1

L-Shaped

Three pieces of each of the four kinds of shape shown below need to be inserted into the grid. Any piece may be turned or flipped over before being put in the grid. No pieces of the same kind can touch, even at a corner. Can you mark in where the Ls are?

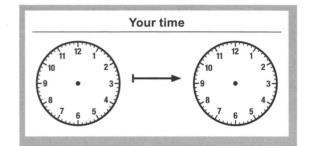

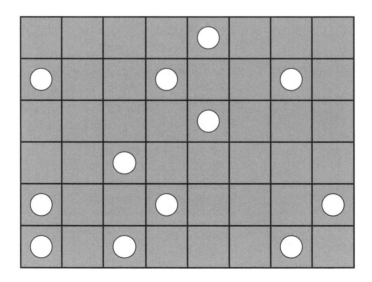

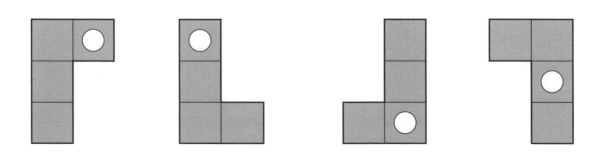

Progressive Matrix

Draw the contents of the missing tile in accordance with the rules of logic already established.

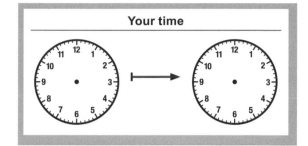

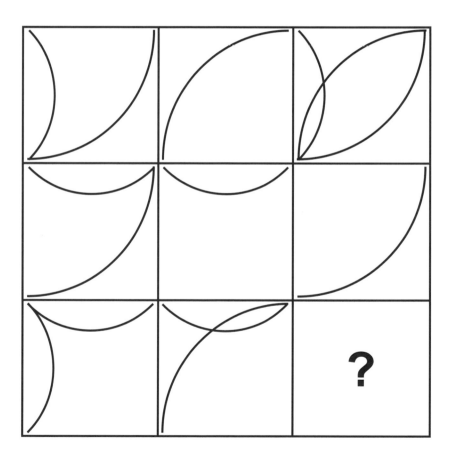

Odd One Out

Study the shapes carefully. Which is the odd one out?

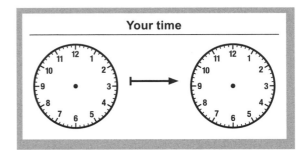

Your time

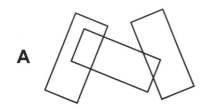

A

B

C

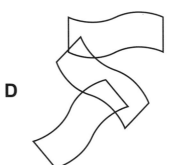

D

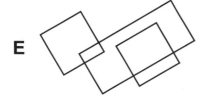

E

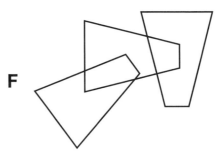

F

THE SOLUTIONS

1

4	2	2	1	1	2
2	1	1	3	3	2
2	1	1	3	3	2
2	4	4	4	4	3
2	4	4	4	4	3
4	1	1	2	2	3

8

1	3	3	3	3	4
4	3	3	1	1	1
4	3	3	1	1	1
1	2	2	1	1	3
1	2	2	1	1	3
2	4	4	3	3	4

2

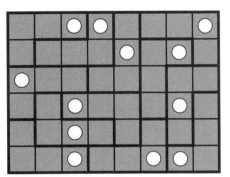

Other solutions may be possible.

9

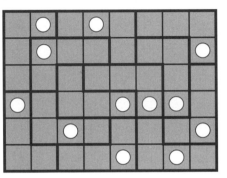

Other solutions may be possible.

3

The triangle moves/points to a different corner clockwise and the white dot moves clockwise one corner at a time.

10

Looking across add a dot in the middle. Looking down remove the large circle and invert the triangle

4

C – In all the others the symbols are in the same order. In C, the black and white dots are swapped round.

11

D – It consists of six lines. B and E pair up with four lines each, and C and A each have five lines.

5

E – The dot moves 45 degrees clockwise and alternates white/black.

12

E – The dot is moving diagonally down one place at a time. When it lies within a figure, that figure is rotated.

6

A

13

C

15

1	2	2	2	2	1
4	4	4	3	3	2
4	4	4	3	3	2
4	1	1	3	3	1
4	1	1	3	3	1
1	3	3	2	2	2

22

4	1	1	3	3	3
2	2	2	1	1	4
2	2	2	1	1	4
3	4	4	4	4	3
3	4	4	4	4	3
2	3	3	2	2	1

16

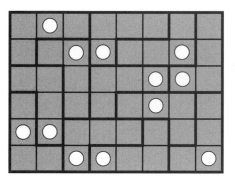

Other solutions may be possible.

23

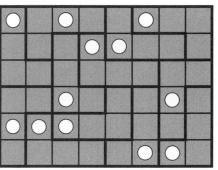

Other solutions may be possible.

17

Looking across add a medium size circle. Looking down remove the large circle.

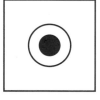

24

Looking at each row across and column down, the lines in the first two tiles are combined to produce the lines in the third tile.

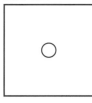

18

D – It has four side branches on the left and three on the right. The rest are the other way round.

19

C – The large arc moves 90 degrees clockwise and the small arc moves 180 degrees.

25

C – The black dot is in circle and square, and the white dot is in triangle and circle. The rest are the other way round.

26

E – The large ellipse moves 45 degrees clockwise. The line moves 90 degrees clockwise within the ellipse and the dot alternates white/black.

27

A

29

3	3	3	4	4	4
3	3	3	1	1	1
3	3	3	1	1	1
1	2	2	2	2	4
1	2	2	2	2	4
3	1	1	4	4	3

36

3	4	4	2	2	1
1	4	4	3	3	1
1	4	4	3	3	1
4	2	2	1	1	4
4	2	2	1	1	4
2	3	3	2	2	4

30

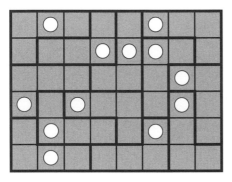

Other solutions may be possible.

37

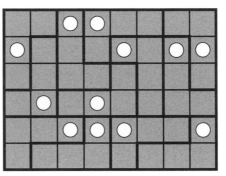

Other solutions may be possible.

31

Each row contains a different symbol, all of which use the same shading, top/middle/bottom in turn.

38

In each row across and column down, the dots appear top middle and bottom in turn.

32

A – B is a mirror image of D and C is a mirror image of E.

39

D – The rest are the same figure rotated.

33

D – The first three figures are being repeated but with only the left half shown.

40

C – The white dot moves two corners clockwise at each stage. The black circle moves one corner clockwise at each stage. In stage three the black circle obscures the white dot.

34

E

43

2	1	1	2	2	3
2	4	4	1	1	3
2	4	4	1	1	3
3	4	4	2	2	2
3	4	4	2	2	2
1	2	2	3	3	2

44

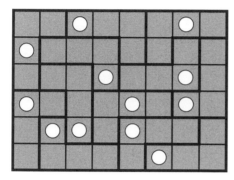

Other solutions may be possible.

45

Looking at each row across and column down, the third tile is produced by combining the contents of the first two tiles, except where two circles appear in the same position in the first two tiles, in which case they are cancelled out.

46

C – A has the same sections as E in reverse (ie top to bottom, bottom to top). B has the same as D.

47

B – The lines form one triangle, then two triangles, then three triangles and, finally, in option B, four triangles.

48

B

50

1	2	2	3	3	2
3	1	1	3	3	4
3	1	1	3	3	4
1	3	3	2	2	2
1	3	3	2	2	2
4	3	3	2	2	4

51

Other solutions may be possible.

52

Working across each row from left to right, add two to each number in the top row, three in the middle row, and four in the bottom row: do the same working down each column, adding three to each number in the left column, four in the middle column and five in the right column.

21

53

E – The rest are the same figure rotated.

54

D – The line is moving clockwise, by one corner, then two corners, then three, then four.

55

C

57

2	1	1	1	1	1
2	3	3	4	4	1
2	3	3	4	4	1
2	4	4	3	3	2
2	4	4	3	3	2
1	4	4	2	2	1

64

1	1	1	4	4	3
3	3	3	2	2	4
3	3	3	2	2	4
4	2	2	1	1	2
4	2	2	1	1	2
3	2	2	3	3	3

58

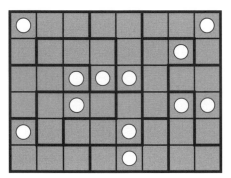

Other solutions may be possible.

65

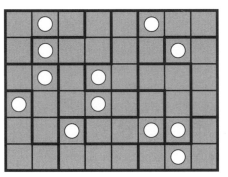

Other solutions may be possible.

59

Looking across, the third tile contains the number of dots arrived at by taking the difference between the number of dots in the first two tiles. Looking down, add the number of dots in the first two tiles to obtain the number of dots in the third tile.

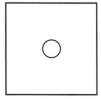

66

Each row across and column down contains a small, medium size and large figure. The top row consists of circles, the second row triangles and the third row squares.

60

B – It is the only one where the arrangement of four lines does not produce any triangles.

67

D - The figure inside has an even number of sides and the figure on the outside has an odd number of sides.

61

C – There are three types of arrow which are repeated. The arrows are moving 45 degrees clockwise at each stage and alternate between being white and having horizontal stripes.

68

A – Each black section moves up its respective column by one position at each stage. After it reaches the top, it then starts again at the bottom.

69

B

71

1	4	4	3	3	2
2	4	4	3	3	4
2	4	4	3	3	4
4	1	1	4	4	2
4	1	1	4	4	2
3	1	1	2	2	3

72

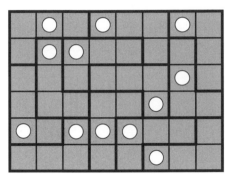

Other solutions may be possible.

73

Each row across and column down contains two different diagonals and a horizontal line.

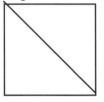

74

B – The rest are the same figure rotated.

75

The arrow moves clockwise by an extra 45 degrees at each stage.

76

D

78

4	3	3	2	2	1
2	3	3	1	1	2
2	3	3	1	1	2
3	1	1	4	4	3
3	1	1	4	4	3
2	2	2	1	1	1

79

Other solutions may be possible.

80

Each row of tiles contains one dot/two dots/ three dots building up from the same starting point.

81

B – D and G are the same figure rotated, as are C and E, H and F, A and I.

82

C – The black dot moves 90 degrees anticlockwise at each stage and the white dot moves 45 degrees clockwise.

85

3	2	2	1	1	1
4	1	1	3	3	2
4	1	1	3	3	2
1	2	2	2	2	4
1	2	2	2	2	4
1	2	2	2	2	3

92

3	3	3	4	4	1
1	2	2	3	3	2
1	2	2	3	3	2
3	2	2	4	4	4
3	2	2	4	4	4
2	3	3	3	3	1

86

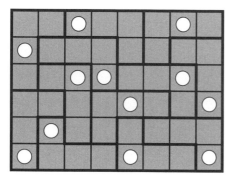

Other solutions may be possible.

93

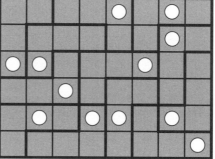

Other solutions may be possible.

87

Looking at each row across and column down, vertical lines are moving right to left and horizontal lines top to bottom.

94

Looking at circles across and down, the third tile is produced by combining the contents of the first two tiles, except where two circles appear in the same position in the first two files, in which case they are cancelled out.

88

A – The rest are the same figure rotated.

95

B – It has a line starting at a corner and facing the middle of a side. The rest have lines pointing to another corner.

89

E – The top and bottom lines move upwards in turn at each stage.

96

B – There are two alternate sequences: in the first, the pentagon is being assembled one side at a time working clockwise, and in the second, the other pentagon is being disassembled one side at a time.

90

D

97

C

99

3	2	2	3	3	3
3	4	4	4	4	1
3	4	4	4	4	1
2	3	3	3	3	4
2	3	3	3	3	4
1	1	1	2	2	1

100

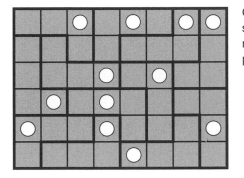

Other solutions may be possible.

101

Looking across each row, the line moves 45 degrees anti-clockwise. Looking down each column, the line moves 45 degrees clockwise.

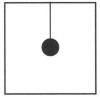

102

C – The rest consist of two identical figures.

103

A – The black dot is moving one side anticlockwise at each stage and alternates outside/inside of the circle. The white dot is moving one side clockwise and alternates inside/outside of the circle.

106

2	2	2	1	1	1
3	3	3	4	4	2
3	3	3	4	4	2
3	1	1	3	3	4
3	1	1	3	3	4
2	4	4	2	2	2

107

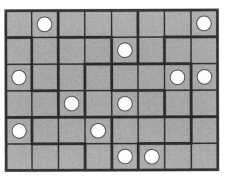

Other solutions may be possible.

108

Working across each row, left to right, move forward three places in the alphabet in the top row, five in the middle row, and seven in the bottom row: do the same working down each column, moving forward four in the left column, six in the middle column and eight in the right column.

109

B – In all the others there are three black and four white dots. In B there are four black and three white.

110

C – The dot is moving down one symbol at each stage. After it has visited and left a symbol, that symbol becomes inverted.

111

E

113

1	4	4	3	3	3
4	2	2	2	2	1
4	2	2	2	2	1
1	1	1	2	2	3
1	1	1	2	2	3
3	2	2	4	4	4

120

1	1	1	1	1	4
2	3	3	3	3	4
2	3	3	3	3	4
3	1	1	2	2	4
3	1	1	2	2	4
2	2	2	2	2	1

114

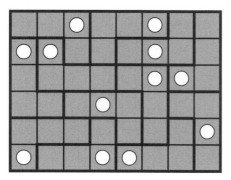

Other solutions may be possible.

121

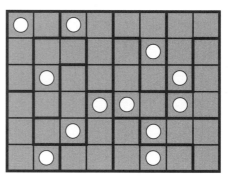

Other solutions may be possible.

115

The top row has wavy lines, the middle row straight lines and the bottom row dots. Each row across and column down contains one, two, and three of each arrangement.

122

In each row across, the hour hand advances by four hours and the minute hand by twenty minutes . In each column down, the hour hand advances by three hours and the minute hand by fifteen minutes.

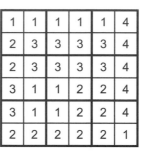

116

D – A is the same as E with black/white dot reversal, and B is the same as C with black/white dot reversal.

123

A – The rest are the same figure rotated.

117

B – The figure alternates between two positions and is white, horizontally striped, white, and vertically striped in turn.

124

D – The first three figures are being repeated in mirror image.

118

D

127

3	1	1	1	1	2
4	3	3	3	3	2
4	3	3	3	3	2
1	4	4	2	2	3
1	4	4	2	2	3
4	4	4	1	1	4

128

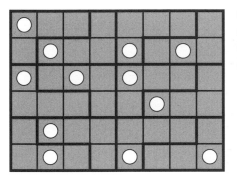

Other solutions may be possible.

129

Each row across and column down has one each of the three different corner line arrangements.

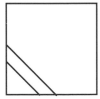

130

D – It has a string of white/white/black/black/white. The rest have a string of white/white/black/white/black.

131

B – The whole figure rotates 90 degrees clockwise at each stage.

132

B

134

3	4	4	3	3	4
1	2	2	3	3	1
1	2	2	3	3	1
3	2	2	2	2	4
3	2	2	2	2	4
2	1	1	1	1	4

135

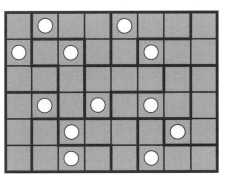

Other solutions may be possible.

136

Looking at each row across and column down, the contents of the final tile are determined by the contents of the first two tiles. Shapes are carried forward from the first two tiles to the final tile, except when shapes appear in the same position in these two tiles, in which case they are cancelled out.

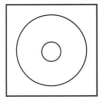

137

E – A is a mirror-image of D, and B is a mirror-image of C.

138

D – The tall figure is moving from left to right one place at a time, behind the others, at each stage.

139

A

141

2	3	3	4	4	4
4	4	4	1	1	3
4	4	4	1	1	3
1	2	2	4	4	1
1	2	2	4	4	1
1	4	4	3	3	2

142

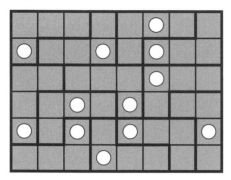

Other solutions may be possible.

143

In each row across and column down there is one black dot. Looking at rows across, the line moves 45 degrees anti-clockwise, looking at columns down, it moves 45 degrees clockwise.

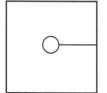

144

D – It is a rounded figure within a straight-sided figure. The rest are straight-sided figures within rounded figures.

145

B – One line is missing at each stage. The missing place moves anticlockwise by an extra place at each stage.

148

4	2	2	1	1	1
2	4	4	2	2	3
2	4	4	2	2	3
3	4	4	1	1	3
3	4	4	1	1	3
3	2	2	1	1	4

149

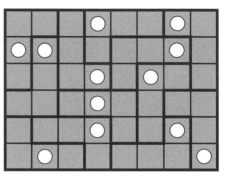

Other solutions may be possible.

150

Looking at each row across and column down, the contents of the final tile are determined by the contents of the first two tiles. Lines are carried forward from the first two tiles to the final tile, except when they appear in the same position in these two tiles, in which case they are cancelled out.

151

D – The rest are the same figure rotated.

152

C – The line moves two places anticlockwise, then one place clockwise. The white dot moves two places clockwise, then one place anticlockwise.

153

D

155

1	3	3	4	4	2
3	2	2	2	2	3
3	2	2	2	2	3
4	2	2	3	3	4
4	2	2	3	3	4
1	1	1	1	1	3

162

2	1	1	2	2	1
2	1	1	4	4	4
2	1	1	4	4	4
4	3	3	3	3	1
4	3	3	3	3	1
2	4	4	2	2	1

156

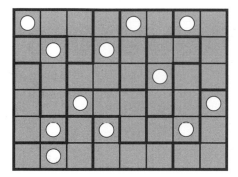

Other solutions may be possible.

163

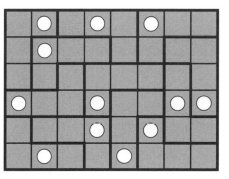

Other solutions may be possible.

157

Looking at each row across, the line moves 45 degrees anti-clockwise. Looking at each column down, the line moves 45 degrees clockwise.

164

Each row across across and column down contains one each of the two different size white circles and a black circle.

158

D – The rest are all the same figure rotated.

165

D – It spirals anti-clockwise from the outside to inside. The others all spiral clockwise from outside to inside.

159

E – The dots are moving right to left and top to bottom respectively. When a dot reaches the end of its line it starts again at the other end of its line at the next stage.

166

C – The pentagon is rotating 180 degrees at each stage and the line is moving from corner to corner at each stage within the pentagon.

160

C

169

3	1	1	3	3	2
2	1	1	4	4	3
2	1	1	4	4	3
4	3	3	2	2	2
4	3	3	2	2	2
1	3	3	4	4	1

176

2	1	1	2	2	2
3	4	4	3	3	1
3	4	4	3	3	1
1	3	3	4	4	4
1	3	3	4	4	4
2	3	3	2	2	1

170

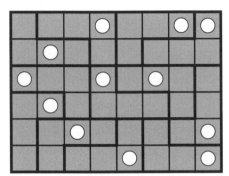

Other solutions may be possible.

177

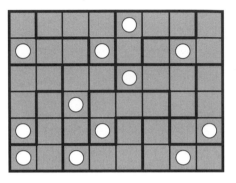

Other solutions may be possible.

171

Looking across add the number of dots in the first two tiles to obtain the number of dots in the end tile. Looking down, subtract.

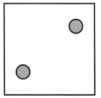

178

Looking across each row and down each column, the contents of the final tile are determined by the contents of the first two. Lines are carried forward from the first two to the final tile, except when they are in the same position in these two tiles, in which case they are cancelled out.

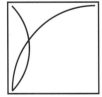

172

C – In all the others the figure on the outside is repeated on the inside.

179

E – It is made up of two squares and a rectangle. All the others are made up from three identical figures.

173

D – The circle left top is alternating white/black/vertical line. The line top right is alternating between two positions. The line bottom left is moving 45 degrees clockwise at each stage. The circle bottom right is alternating black/white.

174

A